It's easy to FIX YOUR BIKE

by John W. McFarlane

"BIKUS NON LUBRIUM BUSTIBUS"
(Aprocryphal Latin Proverb)

GW00600870

W. FOULSHAM & CO., LTD.

New York   Toronto   Cape Town   Sydney

© **1972 John W. McFarlane**
Library of Congress 73-185890
ISBN 0–572–00890–2

CONTENTS

CONTENTS — (Continued)

NOW FOR THE REAL THING

TOOLS, TROUBLES AND FUN

It's Easy to Fix Your Bike

by John W. McFarlane

THIS BOOK doesn't start with choosing a bike. You already have it and it's gone wrong so you bought this book. Maybe you bought it to help care for your bike—good for you!

Here's how to use the book. Flip through it to get acquainted. You already did? Note the simple start—adjusting your saddle and handlebars. We go through tyres and work up to coaster brakes, then on to the complexities of gear hubs and derailleurs. Read the contents list. Read all the pertinent instructions before starting any job. See the tool pages and get the right tools.

If mechanical stuff is new to you, DON'T start by dissecting a helpless coaster brake or derailleur. If your pedals come apart (with a wrench, not abuse) take one apart; clean the bits, grease it, reassemble, and adjust the bearings. It's all shown here.

There is a catch to any repair job. Things don't go just like the book says. Some nuts are rusted on tight, some threads are banged up, bolt heads are so butchered you can't get a wrench on, the wrenches you have are the wrong size, parts are missing, or your bike differs from the pictures. A bike that needs repairs is generally several years old, is second-, third- or fourth-hand, and a bike butcher may have done his worst. So you will have to add your ingenuity to our instructions.

Another catch in a repair job—it may not be right the first time you do it—so go at it again, thinking about it, and charge the extra time to your education. The biggest thing you gain from doing anything new is the ability to do something bigger.

Start to repair something on an old bike, and you get drawn into a string of repairs. You have a flat back tyre, say. Off comes the back wheel to dunk-test the tube. Now you can fix that rattling mudguard—better still, off it comes to take the dents out. Now that the tyre is off you can replace missing spokes—oh yes—and true up the wheel. And now it's easy to get into the brake; it was sluggish anyway. Oh, oh, what a mess! So you clean it up, and find a bad bearing. The chain—it's off, and it seems very dry—so it gets cleaned and oiled. Now you need to repair and replace that chain guard to keep the oil off your pants. The crank bearing seems too loose and dry. So off it comes—more cleaning and greasing.

Let's see—this was to be a 20-minute job on fixing a flat. You did the right thing in fixing the rest. It certainly needed it, and now the bike is easier, more pleasant, and safer to ride. But don't say we didn't warn you! Why did this happen and what should you do? It happened because very few of us give our bikes any attention until something goes wrong. We might as well admit it. This has developed a wonderfully resistant design in bicycles, but even so, it isn't a good idea. An annual overhaul saves a lot of trouble. When we look closely at a neglected bike, it does need lots of attention, even if it still runs. That's why bicycle repairmen want to do more work than you request. They are only being conscientious in putting things right. So—don't get drawn into an overhaul some evening or Sunday if you need the bike next morning. Repairs will take longer than you think and you will need parts—bicycle parts, not makeshifts.

This book can't show the many variations in bicycle parts. The coaster brakes and derailleurs we show typify others so the same instructions apply. If your own bike details appear exactly in this book, well, congratulations!

Now enjoy our program in gorgeous, living black-and-white. No commercials!

SADDLE

Adjusting Height and Tilt

Wrong saddle height tires your legs, wrong saddle tilt keeps you pushing or pulling on the handlebars. Saddle pillars and clamps differ, but they all adjust the same way. Adjust your saddle first for leg length. After adjusting handlebar height, adjust saddle tilt.

Is there a high "sissy bar" behind your saddle? Get rid of it before it gets rid of you. Sometime you will want to get off in the worst way, which you will then do.

Saddle Height

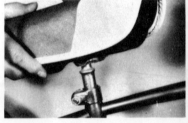

1 To raise or lower the saddle, loosen the seat pillar nut on the bike frame just below the saddle.

2 Stand over your rear wheel, raise or lower the saddle, while twisting it from side to side.

Adjust until your heel, with leg straight, rests on the pedal as you sit squarely on the saddle.

3 Tighten the seat pillar nut very tight, with the right wrench. Don't use pliers, they butcher nuts.

To Tilt or Slide Saddle

1   Loosen the nut on the saddle clamp. This clamp holds the saddle on the saddle pillar. Push the front up if you tend to slide forward.

2   If you have been pulling on the handlebars, push the front of the saddle down to here which is about right. Move it more if needed. Tighten the nut.

"Banana" Saddle

1   Loosen both back stay clamps. If bolts go right through the stays, remove the bolts.

2   Loosen the seat pillar nut. Now you can raise or lower the saddle.

3   Push the saddle up. It may be hard. To tilt it, loosen the saddle clamp.

4   Tighten the saddle pillar nut, and back stay nuts or put bolts in new holes.

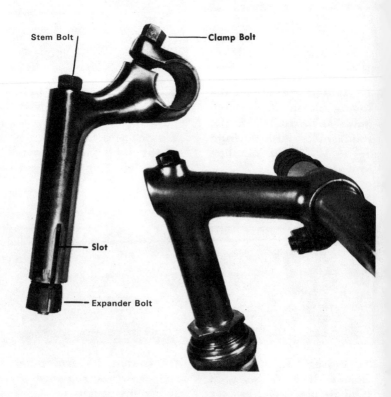

U. S. Type Handlebar Stem   **Continental Type Handle-bar Stem**

Removing A Broken Handlebar Stem

If the handlebar stem seems wobbly or won't stay tight, it is probably broken across the top of the slot. Take the stem bolt out, then the stem. If the stem bolt loosens but won't come out, the broken stem parts may jam the taper plug, so the stem will be hard to pull out. If so, turn the bike over; the stem will come out easier. Then remove one handlegrip, loosen the clamp bolt and take out the handlebar. Get a new stem and put it in.

Adjusting Handlebars

1 To raise or lower, loosen the handlebar stem bolt.

2 Tap the bolt down to drive out the taper plug.

If you loosen the stem bolt so much the plug falls off, pull out the stem, turn the bike over so the plug falls out.

3 Stand over the front wheel, raise or lower the handlebar, twisting it.

4 Tighten the stem bolt; be sure the handlebar is straight across the wheel.

5 To tilt the handlebar, loosen the clamp bolt, tilt the bar, then tighten.

With handlebars and saddle right, you ride so: ball of foot on pedal, knee slightly bent, body leaning forward.

Replacing Handle Grips

Loose handle grips are an invitation to disaster, and bare handlebars are uncomfortable to hold. So do a decent job and use gasket goo cement. Use the type of gasket cement that sets hard, not the other that says soft. Get it at cycle supply stores. If the old grip is still stuck on, slice if off with a knife.

1 Clean and roughen the bar with emery cloth.

2 Apply gasket cement all around the bar.

3 Put cement inside the handle grip also.

4 Push the grip on while you turn it.

5 Make the finger ridges end up underneath.

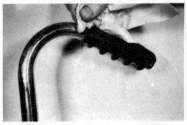

6 Clean off the leftover goo with a paper towel.

Taping Handlebars

Taping is usual on "dropped" handlebars because it permits three different comfortable holds. Tape comes in many delicious colours to match your bike. Rolls are 5 yards, ¾ inch wide, with or without adhesive, none is really needed. Pulled tightly, it will conform even at bends, and stay tight. It shrinks with age (so will you).

1 Start on underside about 2 inches from handlebar stem. Use a bit of sticky tape at the end if needed.

2 Go on wrapping, pulling the tape tight and overlapping about ¼ inch, not more or you'll run short.

3 Tape around the base of the brake lever so your hand won't touch metal. Keep the tape tight.

4 At the open end run the tape right off and cut it. Hold it, stuff the edges in and push in the plug.

If your first job is messy, unwrap and do it over.

Space left over, dammit.

MY! MY!
A FLAT!

Do you suffer from flat tyres, slow leaks, and bad valves? There is hope for you! But not much, unless you fix them. A sudden flat with a large tack in it—this is easy. Leave the wheel on the bike; just get one side of the tyre over the rim, and pull that part of the tube out. A slow leak? Spit-test the valve; if it bubbles, tighten it. If it still bubbles, put in a new one. If it still—no, it won't! But if the valve is okay, then take off the wheel and dunk-test the tube. Wipe off the bubbles and watch for any that come back.

You can take a balloon tyre off with your fingers—don't use tools to pry it off. You may pinch the tube and puncture it. Worse, you may break the wire inside the tyre edge—new tyre coming up! If you have trouble taking the tyre off, it means too much air in the tube or you didn't unstick the tyre from the rim edge. Lightweights need tyre tools in coming off but go back on without.

Before replacing the tyre, be sure the rim is not bent, damaged or badly rusted. Remove rust with a wire brush, and straighten the rim—see Truing a Rim.

Be sure no spokes are sticking into the tube, they will puncture it. File them off and use the rim strip. Center it to cover all spoke nipples, and line up the hole for the valve with the one in the rim.

The talc between the tyre and the tube lets the tyre work around the tube and rim. If the tyre sticks to the tube, the valve stem may pull out.

If you are putting on a new tube or casing, be sure it is the right size for the rim. The tube size is stamped on it and should match the tyre size.

Check your tyres every week with your own tyre gauge, and fill them to the pressure marked on the tyre. Don't use a petrol station hose unless it can be set for the pressure you want. And DON'T ride on soft tyres, it ruins them.

Removing the Tyre

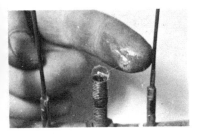

1 Before you assume a puncture, test the valve with spit. If it bubbles, tighten or replace valve.

2 If you see the cause (a tack?) mark both tyre and rim to find the hole in the tube.

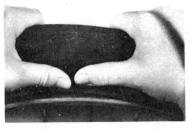

3 Remove the valve stem nut, let the air out (if it isn't already out!).

4 Unstick the tyre from the rim all around so it can go in the rim well.

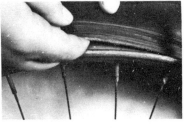

5 At a place opposite to the valve, use your hands to roll the tyre back so you

6 can get your finger under its edge and pull it over the rim.

7 Pull the edge over the rim far enough around so you can pull the tube out.

8 If you know where the puncture is, pull tube out there, otherwise all around

9 Is a valve stem cocked like this? Tube is stuck to tyre, stem will break.

10 Deflate, pull tyre edge off rim, dust talc between tyre and tube. Replace tyre.

Fixing a Puncture

 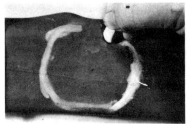

11 If you don't know the puncture location, take off the tube, blow it up and listen for hissing. No hisses? Remove the wheel. Dunk the tube in water, look for bubbles that keep growing.

12 Dry the tube, mark the place with chalk.

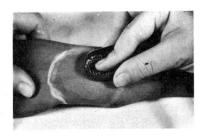 

13 If available, clean with petrol, clean and roughen it with the scraper.

14 Smear with rubber cement, smooth it on with your finger. Let it dry.

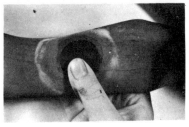

15 Peel the linen off a patch.

16 Squeeze the patch in place.

15

Mounting the Tyre on the Rim

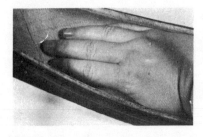

1 Feel for tacks, brambles, etc., all around the tyre.

2 Dust the whole tyre with talc—nice baby!

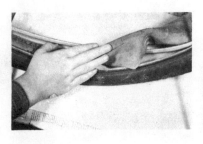

3 Inflate the tube enough to unwrinkle it, stuff it in.

4 Start the rim strip at the valve hole. Talc it.

5 Hold the wheel with its hub against a bench edge, tyre on top, valve near you and inserted in its hole.

6 Start the lower bead, work both ways from the valve, press down on the bead equally with each hand.

7 Some slack should accumulate ahead of your hands. Pop the last bit of lower bead over the rim with your thumb.

8 With the valve pushed in, start the upper bead. Work both ways from the valve as before.

9 If necessary, keep pushing the tube into the tyre so it won't be pinched. Don't use tyre irons.

10 Push the valve in, let it go, to free the tube. If the valve is crooked, hold the spokes, slide the tyre to straighten it.

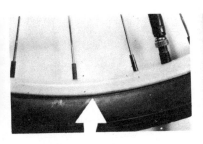

11 Inflate slightly (5 lb.), see if the embossed rim line is visible all around both sides.

12 Bounce the wheel, turning it to free tube kinks. A bit more air, then deflate to arrange tube. Fill and put on the valve cap.

PEDALS

If you are mechanically innocent, make your first victim a pedal—dissect it. If you kill it, replacement is cheap. What you learn about adjusting bearings applies to all others on the bike. Just follow the pictures. Pedals rarely go wrong if they are screwed on tight and if you oil them a few times a season. Neglect kills the bearings and finally the whole pedal. If the treads split, replace them, see 1 and 12. If a right pedal runs loose or a left one tight, the lock nut is loose and the cone needs adjustment. see 9-11. In some pedals the cone is riveted on the spindle, so if the bearings go, get a new pedal. Specify whether right or left, and tread length.

Exploded View of Pedal

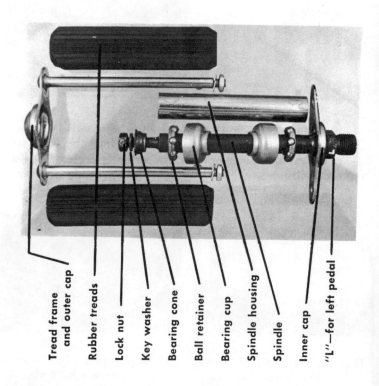

Tread frame and outer cap · Rubber treads · Lock nut · Key washer · Bearing cone · Ball retainer · Bearing cup · Spindle housing · Spindle · Inner cap · "L"—for left pedal

Taking A Pedal Apart

1   Remove the nuts holding the treads. Pull off the outer frame and treads.

2   Loosen and unscrew the lock nut, then unscrew this bearing cone.

3   For a "rat-trap" pedal, remove this cap, then the lock nut.

4   As you unscrew the cone, loose balls, not in cages, fall out both ends.

When you have a pedal apart, clean everything in paraffin with a toothbrush (an old one, paraffin has an awful taste). Replace any bad ball bearings, or complete sets of balls in rat-trap pedals. From here on, the pictures apply mostly to both pedal types. When replacing loose balls, stick them in place with grease.

5   Pick out the ball retainer, pull off the housing and second retainer.

6   Fill ball retainers with ball-bearing lubricant or vaseline.

Reassembling A Pedal

7 Put a retainer FLAT SIDE OUT in each end of the spindle housing.

8 Replace the spindle housing on the spindle. Duck soup, but sticky!

9 Tighten the cone against the ball retainer, then loosen it ¼ turn. This is important.

10 You are now adjusting the bearing clearance. Without turning the cone, add the key washer.

11 Tighten the lock nut. The housing must turn freely. If not, loosen the cone 1/16 turn.

12 Add the tread frame. Outer cap must go over bearing cup (arrow). Add and tighten frame nuts.

Removing A Pedal

The left-hand pedal has a left-hand thread, the right one a right-hand thread. (Just opposite to what seems right.) You need a thin, long, open end 9/16" wrench to get them off. Cycle supply stores sell them for adjusting tappets or something. You may also need penetrating oil.

1 If the thread is stuck with rust, apply a penetrating oil. Let it soak.

2 Loosen a left-hand (left foot!) pedal this way.

3 And start a left pedal on this way. ("L" is stamped near the thread.)

4 Tighten hard—push or pull the wrench in line with the sprocket center.

5 Stripped crank thread? Use a pedal coupling (right or left hand?)

6 If Shorty can't quite reach the pedals, attach blocks sold for the job.

PEDAL CRANK

Nobody loves a crank, but you go around with this one! After a few years neglect, crank bearings may get loose and wear rapidly. If the lock nut loosens, the bearings can tighten and break up. So do a yearly check and greasing.

Two types are common. The one piece type has cones and ball retainers like those of a front wheel axle. The adjusting cone and lock nut have left-hand threads so that turning the crank forward does not tend to loosen them.

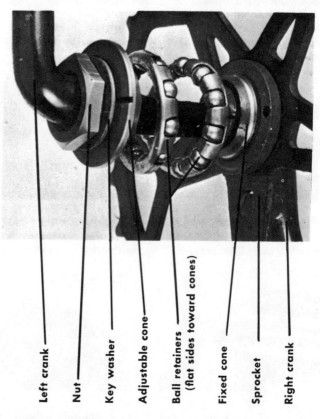

Left crank · Nut · Key washer · Adjustable cone · Ball retainers (flat sides toward cones) · Fixed cone · Sprocket · Right crank

Pedal Crank Parts — 1-Piece Crank

One Piece Crank

1 Holding pedal, loosen lock nut (left-hand thread). Remove pedal.

2 Remove lock washer and bearing cone (left-hand thread).

3 Unseat both ball retainers, pass crank out of bike frame.

4 Clean everything in paraffin, fill ball retainers with ball-bearing grease.

5 Put one greased ball retainer on sprocket, flat side against sprocket.

6 Pass crank back through frame, add the other ball retainer, flat side out.

One-Piece Crank—More

7 Add and tighten bearing cone, finger-tight. Back up 1/4 turn for trial.

8 Tighten lock nut. Check bearing clearance. Loosen lock nut and readjust cone.

Three Piece Crank

9 Loosen nut on taper pin of each crank arm.

10 Run nut out flush with end of taper pin. Tap it with hammer. This loosens pin.

11 Remove nut, pin comes out easily. Loosen notched ring (r-h. thread) Unscrew adjustable bearing race.

12 Remove shaft. Loose balls! Clean everything. Stick balls to bearing surface with ball bearing grease. Put the shaft back.

24

Three-Piece Crank — More

The three piece type has loose balls. The outer part of the bearing is the race; the left one adjusts bearing clearance. Exploded views of both types are shown here.

If you have to replace a broken crank, specify length from crank center to pedal spindle center.

Now, for your annual crank overhaul, be sure to get bearing clearance right. The crank should turn freely with no feeling of bumpiness, but should have enough end play to barely click when pushed sideways.

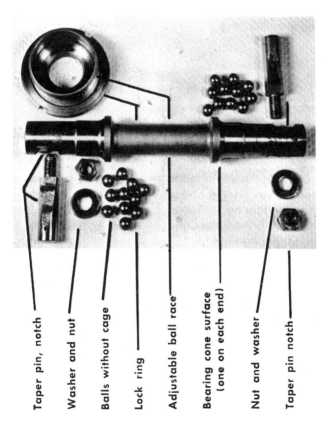

Taper pin, notch — Washer and nut — Balls without cage — Lock ring — Adjustable ball race — Bearing cone surface (one on each end) — Nut and washer — Taper pin notch

Pedal Crank Parts — 3-Piece Crank

Three-Piece Crank—More

13 Now arrange other set of balls in grease in adjustable bearing race. Holding your finger in the hole simplifies this.

14 Screw this bearing race into place around shaft. Tighten it finger tight, back off ¼ turn for trial.

15 Tighten lock ring with hook wrench (if you have one!) Check bearing clearance. Loosen lock ring and readjust as needed.

16 Put in both taper pins (pointing in opposite directions). Pull them in tight by tightening nuts.

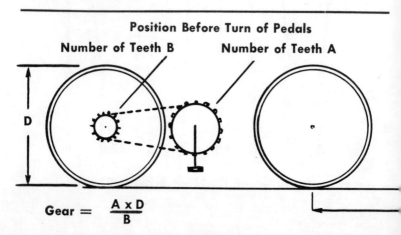

Position Before Turn of Pedals

Number of Teeth B   Number of Teeth A

$$Gear = \frac{A \times D}{B}$$

EASY PEDALING

If your saddle is your height,
And tyres are full inflated,
Your wheel cones aren't too tight,
And chain is lubricated,
Your bike will glide all right
And Corn this will be rated!
           (Translated by Machinery from Russian)

On a one-speed bike you can change the rear sprocket for one with less teeth for more speed, or with more teeth for easier pedaling. Remove the old sprocket—it's easy on a modern bike, see the pages on "Bendix Coaster Brakes." Take the old sprocket to your bike shop to get a new one that will fit. You may need to add a chain link.

The best answer is a bike with multiple speeds—IF you will give your bike good care. Such bikes won't stand kid stuff. But they give easier pedaling OR more speed when wanted. See "3, 5 and 10-Speed Bikes."

The important thing is the ratio of front and rear sprockets, and wheel size. The traditional term for the relation is "gear," and is wheel diameter x no. of front sprocket teeth divided by no. of rear sprocket teeth ("gear" actually works out to the diameter of the equivalent antique bike large wheel). But let's go a step further and state how far the bike goes for one complete turn of the pedals, so we need wheel circumference. This brings in π (pi, but not a la mode). So for a 26-inch wheel, 52- and 20-tooth sprockets we get 26 x 3 1/7 x 52 divided by 20, which is 213 inches. Let's call this "Pace."

Position After One Complete Turn

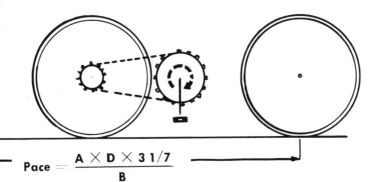

$$\text{Pace} = \frac{A \times D \times 3\,1/7}{B}$$

27

FRONT FORK

Your front fork does not go wrong unless you smack into something, or leave the bike on the driveway behind a car. Then, among other things, the fork gets bent and the bike won't steer well.

While fork bearings don't wear from continuous turning like wheel bearings do, they need cleaning and greasing on the annual overhaul.

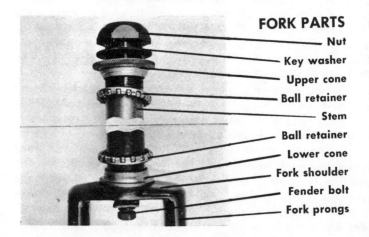

FORK PARTS

Nut

Key washer

Upper cone

Ball retainer

Stem

Ball retainer

Lower cone

Fork shoulder

Fender bolt

Fork prongs

RUNNING INTO SOMETHING bends the fork like this. Steering stability is gone (bike won't steer no hands). Try this: Remove the wheel. Put the axle back in the fork. Turn the fork backwards. Tie a rope from one fork tip, back around the pedal crank hanger and back to the other fork tip. With a stick, twist the two strands of rope together till the fork is pulled back to where it should be. See page 93.

BETTER BUY A NEW FORK! Take in the old one or specify the size and type of wheel and the length of fork from shoulder to top. The tube of the stock fork you will get will be longer. Saw it off squarely to match the old one in length, or assemble it into the bike, leaving off the nut and mark the tube 3/8 inch above the key washer. Then take it out and saw it. The cones, bearings, washer and nut you have will fit.

Greasing the Bearings

To take the fork off, remove the handlebar stem front wheel and mudguard in that order. Then the procedure is quite similar to taking a pedal apart after its rubber treads are off. Unscrew the nut (shown in 3), lift out the key washer, unscrew the cone, drop the fork out, remove upper and lower ball retainers. Clean everything in paraffin, fill the retainers with ball-bearing lubricant. Put it back together in the same order, be sure the flat sides of the retainers face the cones. Adjust the bearing clearance before adding wheel or handlebars. Do it this way:

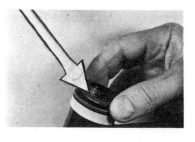

1 Add the cone, tighten it against the ball retainer with your fingers, then unscrew it 1/4 turn.

2 Add the key washer, its lug in the keyway. This washer prevents the nut from turning the cone.

3 Tighten the nut. This moves the cone downward slightly so the nut must be tight when you test the bearing clearance.

4 Try turning the fork. It should rotate freely, but not click when pushed up. If wrong, loosen the nut, tighten the cone 1/16 turn, tighten the nut. Try it again.

FRONT WHEEL

Your front wheel doesn't interest you unless (a) the tyre goes flat; (b) the tyre rubs the fork; (c) an axle nut loosens. If tyre trouble demands removing the wheel, just follow the pictures. If the wheel rubs the fork, loosen one nut, adjust the cone (14,15), center the wheel in the fork, and tighten the nut. If the first nut doesn't do the trick, use the other one the same way. If the wheel is so warped that no axle position prevents the tyre from rubbing the fork, see p. 77. For a loose axle nut, adjust the cone and tighten. Adjusting the cone to get the bearing clearance right is most important. Keep adjusting the cone and trying the wheel after tightening the axle nut, till the clearance is right (See 16).

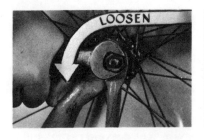

1 Turn the bike upside down. Remove both axle nuts.

2 Even for a small job like this, use a parts can. You won't lose things!

3 Unscrew one cone, use wrenches on both cones if needed.

4 Take out axle, ball retainers, scrub parts and hub in paraffin.

One frequent trouble in taking off a wheel is caused by battered axle threads. Perhaps the first nut comes off easily, but turning the second merely turns the axle. If so, put back the first, tighten it to hold the axle and remove the second. Do likewise to unscrew a cone over a bad thread. NEVER hold the threaded axle by a pliers.

Lock nuts are not usual on most front axles, but if you have lock nuts, adjust the bearing clearance in a vice, as shown for the coaster brakes and omit steps 12, 13. In any case, test bearing clearance as in 14, if there is too much clearance, loosen the nut, tighten the cone 1/16 turn, and tighten the nut again. Keep at it till it's right.

Arrangement of FRONT AXLE PARTS

Two common types are shown here. Lock nuts are not usual, but have been added to the lower axle. Washers, when present, are inside the axle nuts and usually outside the fork. The commonest mistake in putting axle parts back together is getting the ball retainers on backwards.

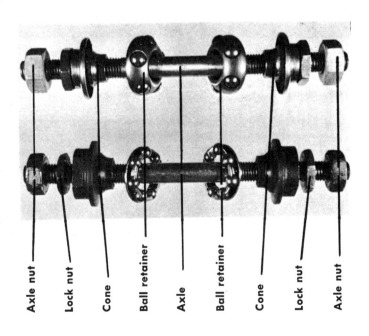

Axle nut   Lock nut   Cone   Ball retainer   Axle   Ball retainer   Cone   Lock nut   Axle nut

Arrangement of Front Axle Parts

Checking and Reassembling the Front Wheel

5 Rough cone surface and worn ball retainer. Get new ones!

6 Grease both ball retainers with ball-bearing lubricant.

7 Screw one cone on ¾", add ball retainer flat side toward cone.

8 Put axle through hub, add second ball retainer flat side out.

9 Add other cone, tighten against ball retainer with fingers.

10 If the fork is an old timer like this, spring it over the axle this way.

While the wheel is off the bike, check it for tacks, slow leaks, etc. If the valve stem is cocked, the tube is sticking to the tyre. Put in talcum powder—see the pages on tyres.

Mounting in the Fork

11 Put the axle back in fork slots. On one side add fender stay, washer and nut.

12 Tighten this one axle nut. Don't tighten the other one just yet.

13 On the other side add the stay, washer and nut. Leave the nut loose.

14 Tighten the bearing cone just finger-tight, back up ¼ turn, hold it.

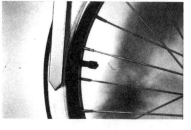

15 While the wheel is held centered in the fork, tighten the nut.

16 The wheel should turn by valve stem weight, but not rattle on the axle.

If the wheel has more than very slight end play on the axle, loosen the nut, tighten the cone about 1/16 turn, tighten the nut, and try it again. Keep at it!

THE CHAIN

The chain must be disconnected to get it off the bike; chains, except those for derailleurs, have removable links for this purpose. Here's how two types work:

1   The plate of this type link is held in the post grooves by springiness.

2   This plate is held on by the split spring lock engaging the post grooves.

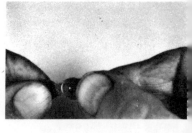

3   Flex the chain to free the link plate, pry it off. Push out the link posts.

4   To reconnect, replace link posts, flex the chain, press the link plate on.

5   To remove, pry off one side of the spring lock at split end, swing it out and

6   lift it off the other post. Lift off the plate and push out the link posts.

DERAILLEUR CHAIN

The chain size for most derailleurs is 3/32" wide by ½" pitch. (What's derailleur? See p. 81). Unlike the usual ⅛" wide chain, derailleur chain has no removable link. To get the chain apart, remove a rivet.

Rivet removing tool in use. Push the rivet out just far enough to unhook the chain by flexing it.

Correct Chain Length

Shimano suggests this: For 5-speed "wide-range" derailleurs, put the chain on the next to smallest sprocket. Chain length is correct when the chain puts the tension roller directly under the guide roller. Use the smallest sprocket if the sprocket cluster is "close-range."

For 10-speed jobs, avoid the chain cage and route the chain directly over the largest front and rear sprockets. With all the slack out, add 2 links for wide range or 4 for close range clusters.

Don't use a new chain on worn sprockets (it won't last) or an old chain on new sprockets. The chainwheel (crank sprocket) can be "revived" by turning it over to use the unworn side of the sprocket teeth. This is also practical with some coaster brake sprockets.

Why Do Chains Break?

1 Front sprocket teeth bent; straighten with a wrench.

2 Bent front sprocket; straighten wih hammer handle through the sprocket.

3 Burrs on sprocket teeth; file them off.

4 Front and rear sprockets misaligned. Most coaster brake sprockets are dished to permit alignment. Washer positions correct on the axle?

5 Bike frame is bent; needs aligning.

6 A 10-speed chain too short for both large sprockets.

OILING THE CHAIN

A dry chain is even worse than a soft tyre in making a bike hard to pedal. The chain needs oil inside the rollers and stick graphite outside—it won't collect grit. The graphite can be applied with the chain in place.

1 If the chain is dirty (it is!), soak and scrub it in paraffin.

2 Blot it on a guest towel (use a rag if you have guests).

3 Dunk all of it in No. 30 oil a few minutes. Hang it to drain overnight.

4 Blot it again, goo the rollers with graphite (cycle supply stores).

Chain draining overnight.

LET'S NOT GET KILLED

The number of bike riders has increased four times since World War II. The number of fatal accidents between bikes and cars is away up. Sadly enough, two thirds of these accidents kill kids 5-14 years old. Traffic is increasing, so are all types of bicycles. Here are the rules for safe bicycling issued by the National Safety Council:

1. Observe all traffic regulations.

2. Keep to the left, as close to the curb as practicable, and ride in a straight line, single file.

3. If you must ride at night, have a white headlight in good working· order and a red light on the rear of the bike. Wear white or light-coloured clothing.

4. Have and use a horn or bell for signaling.

5. Always give pedestrians the right of way.

6. Watch for parked cars pulling out into traffic and for car doors that open suddenly.

7. Never hitch onto other vehicles, stunt or race in traffic.

8. Never carry riders.

9. Be sure your bike is in safe mechanical condition.

10. Slow down at all intersections.

11. Use proper hand signals turning, stopping, or slowing.

YOUR BIKE WILL BE STOLEN

Many are. The ones that aren't are locked by a heavy chain through the frame, the back wheel and a bike rack or pole. The chain is a type that can't be cut by bolt cutters. Record your bike's serial number — it is usually just above the rear wheel axle or just above the front fork.

THE BACK WHEEL

Getting the Wheel Off

Let's say you want to mount a new tyre, or find a puncture. So the wheel must come off. Turn your bike upside down, with the back mudguard resting on a box. Don't dissect your bike on the lawn—lost parts get into the lawnmower, so put any loose parts in a can.

While the wheel is off, clean the hub, replace any needed spokes, fix and tighten the mudguard clean and oil the chain. Now follow the pictures.

Putting the Wheel Back On

Important things in putting on a back wheel:

1. Bearing clearance

2. Wheel centered in fork

3. Correct chain tension

4. Mudguard centered over wheel

The bearing clearance can and should be adjusted while the wheel is off if the brake has a lock nut on both sides—see the coaster brake pages. These lock nuts are large, thin ones—if missing, get them.

Chain tension can be a problem on a cheap bike. The tension changes as the crank turns because the big sprocket is a bit eccentric (aren't we all?)

1 Undo the brake arm nut, hold it, unscrew the bolt. Don't lose them!!

2 Loosen both axle nuts. On a derailleur, first put chain on smallest sprocket.

3 Lift the wheel out. No need to disconnect the chain on a modern bike.

4 Hold chain up, replace wheel in frame. Attach brake arm clip loosely.

5, 6 For coaster brake bikes: tighten the axle nuts loosely. Turn the pedals to see if chain is tighter at one position. If so, tighten axle nuts there so chain can move ½ inch. Tighten the axle nuts so they center the wheel in the frame. Now tighten the brake arm clip.

The wheel should now turn freely, but not rattle on the axle. To cure more than slightest sideways play, loosen axle and lock nut, sprocket side, tighten the cone 1/16 turn, tighten the nuts. Keep at it.

HOW A COASTER BRAKE WORKS

A coaster brake is in the rear wheel hub. It can drive forward, coast, or apply a brake. In the hub is a large "driving screw" attached to the sprocket. On the large, fast thread of this screw is a loosely fitting clutch. When the sprocket is turned forward, a slight drag between clutch and stationary axle makes the clutch run up the thread toward the sprocket. The clutch wedges itself against the inside of the hub shell so that the hub and wheel turn with the sprocket. So the bike drives forward.

When the sprocket is turned backward, the drag between clutch and axle makes the clutch run down the thread, away from the sprocket. Teeth (dentils) on the left end of the clutch engage teeth on a brake part, pushing it to apply the brake. In "shoe brakes," two cones are pushed together to expand shoes against the inside of the hub shell, as in Bendix, Komet, etc. In a "disc brake" a pile of discs are squeezed together. Some fit the hub shell and turn with it. Interleaving discs are held stationary on the axle. Mattatuck, and its ancestor, New Departure, use discs.

The brake arm holds the hub from turning when the brake is on.

The drag against the clutch makes it act as it should. The drag must be greater than the friction of the clutch on its thread. If there were no drag, the clutch would just turn with the sprocket, and not run along the thread. Then it would not either drive or brake. The drag in most cases is exerted by a spring linking the clutch and a non-rotating part.

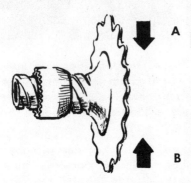

When a sprocket turns in direction A, clutch part moves to the left and engages the brake.

When sprocket turns in direction B, clutch part moves to the right and engages the hub shell to drive forward.

Action of clutch on driving screw.

Brake shoes loose | Hub shell engaged by driving clutch

Driving ↗

Brake shoes expanded by cones against hub shell

Braking ↘

Typical Shoe Brake — Bendix RB-2

Brake cylinder (Komet, Jet, etc.) expanded by squeezing tapered end parts together, rubs inside of hub shell.

Discs loose | Hub shell engaged by driving clutch

Driving ↗

Fixed and moving brake discs compressed by clutch sleeve

Braking ↘

Typical Disc Brake — Mattatuck

41

Lubricating Your Brake

Coaster brakes, as they come from the factory, are lubricated and will work well for a long time. If the brake is used a lot, it should be oiled through the oil cap on the hub shell (if present) twice a season with motor oil, SAE 20 or 30. If the brake is used in hilly country, oiling is needed oftener, even monthly. Don't use a lot of oil, and, above all, don't use light household or gun oils, or the grease will be washed out of the brake.

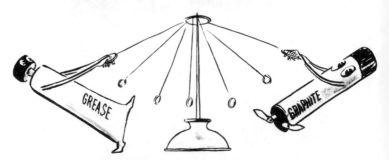

After several seasons (one season for a very active bike) the brake needs cleaning and relubricating. If you aren't smart with gadgets don't tackle it yourself. Do your mechanical teething on something cheap like a pedal.

The following pages show how to take apart and relubricate the most popular brakes. The most important parts to lubricate are the ball bearings. Lubricant for ball bearings must not be so firm that the balls "channel" it (cut holes) and get no more on them, or so liquid that it soon runs out. So use a ball bearing lubricant such as that sold in tubes for bicycle work. Grease sold for car front-wheel bearings is a bit heavy but will do.

> There was once a sad sack who loved biking
> But never found oil to his liking.
> Now the cost of repair
> Has him tearing his hair,
> And his shoe leather sizzles from hiking.

About Bearing Clearance—All ball bearings on a bike are adjusted by a "cone" which bears the inner surface on which the balls run. This surface is more or less cone shaped, so that screwing one cone toward the other tightens the whole bearing. The cone meant for adjustment has flat surfaces on its outside to take a wrench. A thin wrench is needed. Cones are shown in all the exploded views of brakes and other parts.

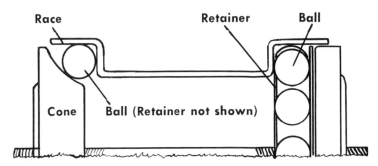

Race   Retainer   Ball

Cone   Ball (Retainer not shown)

The bearing clearance is more important than you think. If too loose, there may be a 300-lb. pressure on each ball in turn. If too tight, all the balls are under terrific pressure. In either case, the cones will wear, and then the balls will smash up. The cone must be held tightly in place by its lock nut or axle nut. Lock nuts simplify adjusting the bearing clearance, and are highly desirable. Adjusting the bearing clearance is a little tricky, but not really hard. The axle should turn freely with no feeling of bumpiness, and it should always be tried with the lock nut tightened down, because the lock nut pushes the cone in slightly. This is shown in detail in the pictures that follow.

We assume that you have a vice. To clamp things like axles and driving screws without damage, cover the jaws with sheet copper. Unlike human false teeth, these jaws will not dent things.

Ready for a brakectomy? Operations on four popular brakes follow. There are many others, usually similar to one shown here. If the brake axle has a square end, follow the Komet Super routine. Otherwise follow Bendix or Centrix. New Departure (old, but good) resembles Mattatuck. If the brake is strange, put the parts on a rod or wire as you take them out, to keep them in order and right side to. Good luck!

So You Want To Fix It!

Look over the pictures and get an idea of what you are tackling. If you haven't done mechanical work before, don't start here.

Put all the parts in a can of paraffin as you take them off, or you will spend an hour looking for them afterwards. Scrub all the parts with a toothbrush (an old one, paraffin tastes awful!). When the parts are clean, dry them on paper towels, or in an air blast from a pump.

The main things in overhauling any brake are these:

1. Replace broken or worn parts.
2. Clean everything thoroughly.
3. Use grease and oil as required.
4. Get the parts back in the right places.
5. Get the ball retainers right side out.
6. Adjust the bearing clearance correctly.

You can get replacement kits on all internal parts for some brakes, including Bendix.

Is the Brake Hard to Apply?

Look for a rough expander surface (left). These fine ridges add too much friction when the brake cylinder is pushed onto this expander. Smooth this conical surface (right) with emery cloth—easy on a lathe. Wash all grit away in paraffin. A "moly" grease also reduces friction on this surface.

Nasty Things That Happen

Pedals don't take hold forwards at once if at all, or slip.

- Broken or weak retarder spring, replace or bend retarder inwards.
- Clutch tapered surface worn smooth—replace.
- Gummy grease or grit on driving screw. Clean it and use oil.
- Damaged thread on driving screw or clutch—replace.
- Very loose bearing cone. Adjust for very slight end play.

Pedals don't engage brake at once, if at all.

- Broken or weak retarder spring—see above.
- Dentils (teeth) filled with dirt or stripped—replace.
- Brake arm not properly on stationary cone. Fix it!

Slow brake action.

- Polished hub inside. Roughen with coarse emery cloth.
- Polished brake shoes. Roughen, or replace if worn.
- Brake cone surface is rough—see opposite page.

Brake won't release, or drags.

- Bearing cone too tight. Adjust it for very slight end play.
- Bent axle—replace it.

Brake squeals.

- Worn brake shoes—replace.
- Somebody "improved" things with petrol or paraffin. Clean out, use right grease and oil.

Cracking or grinding noises.

- Broken or worn balls, cones or races—replace.
- Chain too tight, dry, worn, or partly broken. Adjust, oil, or replace.
- Worn chain on new sprocket—get new chain.
- Dust caps damaged or put on wrong.

Too much motion between driving and braking.

- Bearing cone too loose, or bearing at brake arm end is not seated.
  Do something, don't just stand there!

45

BENDIX COASTER BRAKES

Including the "70," there have been 6 models, all effective, simple and backed by widely available parts and service. Models are listed here, and most are identified on

	Axle Nut	Axle Washer	Lock Nut	Arm Clip		Brake Arm	Dust Cap, Arm Side	Ball Retainer	Brake Expander, Anchor End	Brake Shoe Keys	Brake Shoes	Brake Expander, Drive End	Retarder Spring	Driving Clutch	Retarder Sub Assy.
1st Model	BB	13A	14A	15	11	10	32	16	33	51	22	6			3
RB-1	BB	13A	14A	15	11	10	32	16	59	51	22	56		112	53
Junior	BB	13A	14A	15	11	10	32	16	233		222			112	259
RB-2	BB	13A	14A	15	11	10	32	16	133		22			112	159
70J	BB	13A	14A	15	11	610	532	516	633		222			112	659
70	BB	13A	14A	15	11	510	532	516	533		22			112	159

Notes on Bendix Models

All models have two brake shoes except Junior and 70J which have one each.

The 1st Model and RB1 had two separate brake shoe keys instead of integral lugs on the brake expanders.

The hub shell part number depends on the number of spoke holes and gauge of the spoke holes.

The sprocket part numbers depend on the number of teeth. The sprocket of the 1st model goes on with a right-hand thread, its locking ring has a left-hand thread. The RB-1 sprocket fits on splines. The others have three lugs and a spring ring retainer.

the brake arm. The drawing shows the "70," pictures apply to "70" and RB-2, and in general to all models. Junior models, for 16" and 20" bikes, have one brake shoe. The 70J differs internally from the 70 mainly in its one brake shoe and expanders. The same applies to the Junior and RB-2.

Exploded View—Bendix 70 Coaster Brake

Hub Shell	Axle	Ball Retainer	Drive Screw	Ball Retainer	Adjusting Cone	Locknut	Dust Cap, Sprocket	Sprocket	Retaining Ring, Sprocket	Axle Washer	Axle Nut
	4	16	2	20	7	15	31	44-48	5	14A	13A
	4	16	52	20	7	15	158	60-64	55	14A	13A
81-87	4	16	102	20	7	15	158	142-148	155	14A	13A
81-87	4	16	102	20	7	15	158	142-148	155	14A	13A
581-586	4	516	502	20	7	15	558	142-148	155	14A	13A
581-586	4	516	502	20	7	15	558	142-148	155	14A	13A

Prefix letters BB are used on the above part numbers.

All Bendix brake parts should be ordered through a bicycle dealer. Bendix does not accept direct orders.

Taking a Bendix Brake Apart

1 Hold cone with wrench. With another, loosen and remove the lock nut.

2 Remove cone. If axle thread has battered spots, use a wrench.

3 Unscrew the sprocket. Lift out the ball retainers in it and under it.

4 Lift the wheel off the rest of the brake. Things fall out when you do!

5 Take away the brake shoes and lift off the clutch assembly. Dirty, isnt it!

6 Pull the driving clutch out of the retarder-brake clutch assembly.

Two Bendix repair kits have all parts except hub shell and sprocket. Kit BB-121 fits RB-1, RB-2, and Junior (any smooth hub shell with groove). Kit BB-521 fits '70 and 70J (knurled hub shell).

Checking for Wear

1 Check this and other bearing surfaces for rough areas, cracks, or pits. Check ball bearings also.

2 If these driving clutch serrations are worn smooth replace entire assembly (clutch, expander, spring).

3 If brake shoes have a high polish, roughen them with emery cloth. If badly worn, replace them.

4 If the retarder spring exerts only a very light drag, squeeze it together to give it more "bite."

Taking a Sprocket Off Its Driver

1 To remove a sprocket either tap it off, see p. 66 or release the spring ring with a sharp point.

2 Getting the ring back on (without the right tool) can be done with one or two screwdrivers. Patience!

The sprocket of the 1st model screwed onto the driver with right-hand thread. Lock ring had left-hand thread.

Lubricating and Reassembling Bendix

1   Pack all ball retainers with ball-bearing grease. Also grease brake cones and shoes, retarder spring, clutch face and smooth part of axle.

2   Use oil (30 SAE) on the driving screw threads.

3 Screw this brake shoe expander this far on the axle.

4 Using the dust cap, push the ball retainer into place, flat side against the cap.

5 Add the brake arm, name side out. Add and tighten the lock nut.

6 Slip the retarder spring over this expander, and over the driving clutch.

7 Put this expander-clutch assembly on the axle, raised lugs in line. Older brakes used keys here.

8 Add the two brake shoes, seated against the expander lugs (or older keys).

9 Hold brake shoes; enter the whole hing in the hub from the big-hole side.   Junior Model ▲

10 If it stops part way (upper) raise the axle slightly to let the balls drop into place (lower).

11 Holding axle tightly in hub, turn wheel over, put in the large ball retainer, flat side out.

12 Screw in the sprocket, add the small ball retainer. All ball retainers must be flat side out.

13 Add the cone, tighten it with your fingers, unscrew it 1/4 turn.

14 Hold the cone so it can't turn, add and tighten the lock nut.

The "unscrew 1/4 turn" is a trial setting for bearing clearance. It may be too loose. Make further 1/16 turn adjustments, tightening the lock nut each time. Clearance is right when there is very slight end play and the wheel rotates freely.

KOMET SUPER COASTER BRAKE
Also Torpedo Boy

This brake has a single split cylinder for its braking surface. It is expanded against the hub shell by conical expanders in its ends. Springiness of the (stationary) cylinder on the (rotating) clutch provides the needed drag. Note the squared axle end and method of bearing adjustment—different from other brakes.

Taking it Apart

If your Komet Super needs attention, take it apart so:

1 Loosen and remove lock nut on the brake arm.

2 Hold axle by squared end. Use brake arm to unscrew brake cone.

3 Unscrew it right off the axle.

4 Remove sprocket. Clean all parts in kerosene.

Checking for Condition

If the brake is hard to apply, either the brake cylinder is worn smooth, or the stationary brake cone is rough, see p. 44. Roughen the cylinder with emery cloth or better still, replace it. Smooth the brake cone, as on p. 44. If worn to a polish, roughen the hub shell interior.

Also replace a driving clutch that is worn smooth.

Exploded View

x T 93 A	Spindle Nut (2 pieces)
x K 102 A	Lock Nut
x T 77	Lock Washer
x K 108	Brake Arm
x T 74	Clip, complete
x 74 d*	Bolt and Nut for Clip
K 161/2 A	Cone with Ball Bearing and Dust Cap
x K 113	Brake Cylinder
x K 107	Driving Cone

K 161/3	Hub Shell
x K 110 A	Axle with Cone (packed into Polythene bag)
K 161/4	Ball Bearing S 1025 on Inner Hub Barrel
K 161/5	Inner Hub Barrel, complete
K 161/5a*	Ball Bearing S 1025 in Inner Hub Barrel
x K 112a*	Dust Cap in Inner Hub Barrel
K 161/6	Dust Cap on Inner Hub Barrel
x 617	Sprocket, snap-on type, 14-22 teeth
x 616e	Lock Spring (for sprocket, snap-on type)

x parts may also be used for Komet Coaster Hub (old style)
x »A« means that part has American thread.)
* no illustration.

53

Checking Komet Super — More

Check the surfaces on which all ball bearings run. If any are pitted, cracked, or rough, replace the part concerned. Also check ball retainers for rough or broken balls. If in doubt put in new ball retainers.

Lubrication

Pack the ball retainers with ball-bearing grease, also apply it to the brake cylinder, and fill the cylinder with it for a reserve supply. If the brake must be used a lot in hilly country, use a heat-resistant grease such as Texaco Starfax No. 2 on the brake cylinder. Put grease inside the driving screw and oil, SAE 20 or 30 on its threads.

Put grease on the knurled surface of the driving clutch. and on the friction area where it enters the brake cylinder. Add oil through the oiler twice yearly.

Putting it Together

1 Put driving **clutch** into plain (not notched) end of brake cylinder.

2 Add larger ball retainer to brake cone, flat side away from cylinder, and add cylinder.

3 Put this assembly in hub shell—it will only go in one side.

4 Grease other ball retainer and put it flat side out in other side of hub.

5 Add and screw sprocket in, holding brake cone in.

6 Add axle and screw it all way into brake cone.

7 Add dust cap to brake cone.

8 Add brake arm, name side out.

9 Add notched washer.

10 Add but don't tighten lock washer.

11 Hold brake arm, adjust bearings, as shown below.

12 Don't let axle or arm turn, tighten lock washer.

55

Adjusting Bearings with Wheel in Bike Frame

13 With the pedals held, the wheel must roll freely. If there's more than 1/8'' side play at the rim of the wheel, tighten the bearings. If there's no side play, loosen up. You can do this with the wheel in the bike frame. Loosen the axle nuts on both sides, and the locknut on the brake arm side.

14 Screw squared end of the shaft in finger-tight, back off 1/4 turn. This is a trial setting.

15 To prevent axle from turning and changing adjustment, tighten the right-hand axle nut.

16 Tighten brake arm lock nut, and axle nut. Check for free wheeling and side play. Now readjust it!

If you don't have the intended hook wrench to fit this notched washer, you can get a small hinged (adjustable) hook wrench from tool supply stores.

SACHS JET COASTER BRAKE

This brake succeeds the Komet Super, is similar to it, and the same procedure applies. Since the bearing cone is fixed on the axle must be turned relative to the brake arm to adjust bearings. But the axle lacks a square end, so, loosen both axle nuts and the brake arm lock nut. Then turn the axle with a pliers, first covering it with copper tubing to protect the threads.

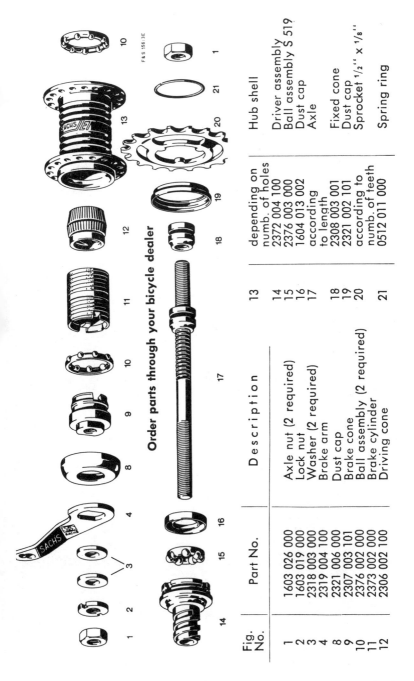

Order parts through your bicycle dealer

Fig. No.	Part No.	Description
1	1603 026 000	Axle nut (2 required)
2	1603 019 000	Lock nut
3	2318 003 000	Washer (2 required)
4	2319 004 100	Brake arm
8	2321 006 000	Dust cap
9	2307 003 101	Brake cone
10	2376 002 000	Ball assembly (2 required)
11	2373 002 000	Brake cylinder
12	2306 002 100	Driving cone
13	depending on numb. of holes	Hub shell
14	2372 004 100	Driver assembly
15	2376 003 000	Ball assembly S 519
16	1604 013 002	Dust cap
17	according to length	Axle
18	2308 003 001	Fixed cone
19	2321 002 101	Dust cap
20	according to numb. of teeth	Sprocket 1/2" x 1/8"
21	0512 011 000	Spring ring

F & S 156 3E

57

CENTRIX AND PERRY B-500 COASTER BRAKES

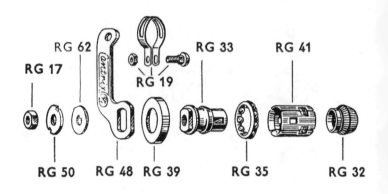

RG 17 RG 62 RG 19 RG 33 RG 41

RG 50 RG 48 RG 39 RG 35 RG 32

Taking It Apart

1 Loosen axle nuts, lift wheel out of bike frame.

2 Unscrew and remove the adjusting cone.

3 Unscrew and lift out the sprocket.

4 Lift wheel off rest of brake. Messy, huh?

The Centrix and Perry B-500 coaster brakes are much alike. They both expand a cylinder against the hub shell for their braking action, and both have a cone-shaped clutch on a screw for their forward drive. They both can be taken apart and put together the same way. So we group them together here.

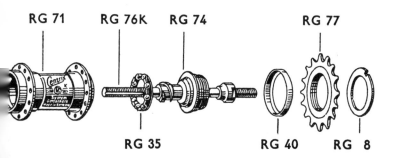

RG 71   RG 76K   RG 74   RG 77

RG 35   RG 40   RG 8

Exploded View — Centrix

Checking and Lubricating

Clean everything in paraffin with a toothbrush. Look for worn, pitted, cracked or broken parts. Replace the brake cylinder if worn smooth. If any surfaces on which ball bearings run are pitted or rough, replace the part concerned. If any balls are chipped, replace the whole ring. If the brake was hard to apply, try smoothing the brake cone surface, see p. 44.

The Centrix brake cylinder has four parts, hooked together by springs. If even one of these springs is broken, the cylinder drags on the hub shell. More important, the cylinder no longer retards the driving cone. Result — uncertain driving and braking.

LUBRICATING. Pack the ball retainers with ball-bearing grease, include the balls inside the driver. Also grease the outside of the driving cone (traveller), inside and outside of the brake cylinder, and smooth part of the axle. Use light oil on driver threads.

Putting It Together

5 Screw brake cone back on 1 ¼ inch, if it was off.

6 Add the dust cap, arm, space washer if any, lock washer, and lock nut.

7 Add greased ball retainer and brake cylinder so its catches fit holes in brake cone.

8 Add the driving cone. It has no retarder spring, cylinder supplies needed spring action.

9 Push whole thing into hub, large hole side.

10 Add other greased ball retainer, flat side out.

The Perry B-500 brake does have a retarder spring on the driving cone. Its brake cylinder also differs from the Centrix cylinder, but assembles similarly.

11 Screw sprocket into place, after greasing its small bearing.

12 Screw bearing-adjusting cone in finger-tight, back off ¼ turn.

14 Now adjust bearing clearance. Start with ¼ turn back-up, and tighten right axle nut. The wheel should roll freely, with 1/16 - 1/8″ side play at the rim. Readjust till it does. Don't let cone turn when you position wheel for proper chain tension. Chain should move about 1/2″ at its middle.

13 Put wheel back in bike frame and tighten left axle nut.

15 If sprocket itself was off, drop it on to engage notches.

16 Add spring ring—easy with two screw drivers.

The sprocket of older brakes was screwed onto the driver, with a right-hand thread. It was locked on with a notched ring, threaded on with a left-hand thread. Newer sprockets are held as shown here.

SHIMANO COASTER BRAKE

This is an expanding shoe brake of conventional design. In dismantling and servicing it is rather similar to the Centrix brake. So follow the Centrix instructions. Note that the retarder spring (clutch spring) has a tab that fits the slot between halves of the brake shoes.

Item No.	Part No.	Description
1	2812200	Hub Nut
2	2822600	Lock Washer
3	2812100	Lock Nut
4	2810500	Hub Cone
5	3219022	Ball Retainer A & Balls
6	3212000	Snap Ring C
7	2822000	Dust Cap R
8	2821300	Driver
9	2829005	Ball Retainer C & Balls
10	2829001	Hub Shell 28 Holes
11	2821400	Clutch Cone
12	2822500	Clutch Spring
13	2821500	Brake Shoe
14	2822300	Shoe Spring

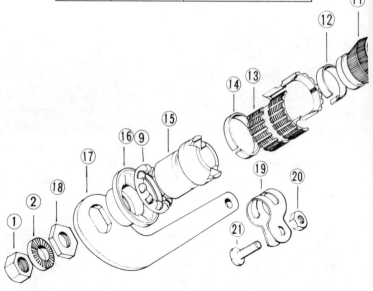

Exploded View and Parts List

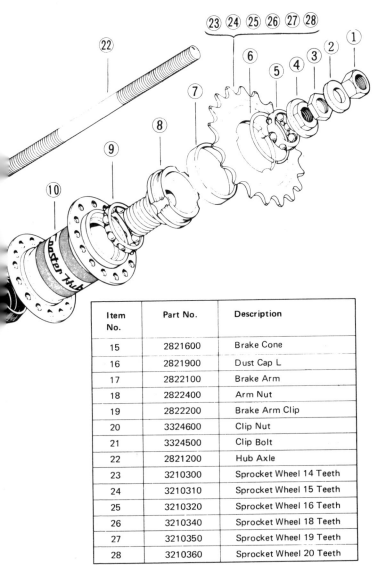

Item No.	Part No.	Description
15	2821600	Brake Cone
16	2821900	Dust Cap L
17	2822100	Brake Arm
18	2822400	Arm Nut
19	2822200	Brake Arm Clip
20	3324600	Clip Nut
21	3324500	Clip Bolt
22	2821200	Hub Axle
23	3210300	Sprocket Wheel 14 Teeth
24	3210310	Sprocket Wheel 15 Teeth
25	3210320	Sprocket Wheel 16 Teeth
26	3210340	Sprocket Wheel 18 Teeth
27	3210350	Sprocket Wheel 19 Teeth
28	3210360	Sprocket Wheel 20 Teeth

MATTATUCK COASTER BRAKE
Also New Departure

The Mattatuck coaster brake continues and improves on the old New Departure coaster brake. Both use multiple discs for braking. This means that all the braking wear is taken on the discs, which can be replaced easily and cheaply.

New Departure model D brakes take Mattatuck parts. Use the Mattatuck Clutch Service Set to replace the N.D. clutch sleeve, brake clutch, and transfer spring (no more broken springs!). Use the Driver Service Set to replace the N.D. driver, sprocket (how many teeth?) and related parts. Otherwise all parts fit, including the brake disc set.

Taking It Apart

1   Hold the cone, loosen and remove the lock nut.

2   Unscrew and remove the cone.

3   Unscrew and remove the sprocket.

4   Lift the wheel off rest of brake parts. Mess!

Checking for wear: In addition to the points on p. 45, check the brake discs for damage or bad wear.

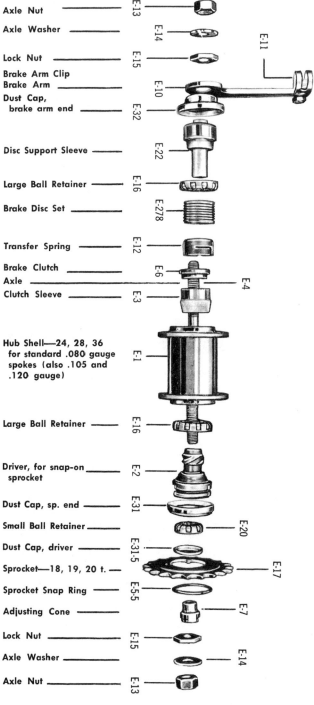

Axle Nut — E-13

Axle Washer — E-14

E-11

Lock Nut — E-15

Brake Arm Clip
Brake Arm — E-10

Dust Cap,
  brake arm end — E-32

Disc Support Sleeve — E-22

Large Ball Retainer — E-16

Brake Disc Set — E-278

Transfer Spring — E-12

Brake Clutch — E-6
Axle — E-4
Clutch Sleeve — E-3

Hub Shell—24, 28, 36
for standard .080 gauge
spokes (also .105 and
.120 gauge) — E-1

Large Ball Retainer — E-16

Driver, for snap-on
  sprocket — E-2

Dust Cap, sp. end — E-31

Small Ball Retainer — E-20

Dust Cap, driver — E-31-5

Sprocket—18, 19, 20 t. — E-17

Sprocket Snap Ring — E-5-5

Adjusting Cone — E-7

Lock Nut — E-15

Axle Washer — E-14

Axle Nut — E-13

65

Taking Apart a Mattatuck Brake—continued

5 Lift off clutch parts, brake discs and ball bearing.

6 Leave this all assembled unless this surface is rough.

7 Pull clutch sleeve out of transfer spring.

8 Turn brake clutch in transfer spring, using disc sleeve. Then expel clutch with it.

9 Pry out this dust cap carefully, to reuse it. Lift out bearing under it.

10 Clamping driver, tap sprocket with light hammer. Snap ring flies off!

The sprocket needs to come off the driver only if you want to change sprockets or to replace the driver because of wear on the bearing surface or damage to the thread. When you clamp the driver, use copper covers on the vice jaws. Watch that snap ring, or put a loop of wire or string through and around driver and sprocket to trap it.

Lubricating and Reassembling

1 Clean and grease the interior of the hub.

2 Pack all bearings with grease. Add a large one at arm end, flat side at arm.

3 Oil the brake discs with h y p o i d lubricant (available at petrol stations).

4 Add discs, first alternate with the last one

5 Grease t h e b r a k e clutch, a n d outside of clutch sleeve. Put oil on sleeve threads.

6 Add the t r a n s f e r spring, push in the brake clutch, push in the clutch sleeve.

The transfer spring's flat side goes against the discs, the brake clutch teeth face out to engage clutch sleeve teeth.

Use oil on the discs, grease drags too much. If the brake squeals add **ONE**, just one drop of castor oil.

Assembling Mattatuck Brake—continued

7 Line up the brake disc lugs with a straight edge. They go in the hub easier clamped—see below.

8 Slide the large hole side of the hub over the brake discs, lining up the lugs with the hub splines.

9 Add the other bearing, flat side out.

10 Add the small bearing to the sprocket, and its dust cap. Put in the sprocket.

11 Add and finger-tighten the cone, back off ¼ turn.

12 Without letting axle or cone turn, tighten lock nut.

Bearing clearance is important. Keep adjusting the cone 1/16 turn and locking it until there is very slight end play.

Brake discs go into the hub easier if clamped with a 2¼″ piece of ½″ water pipe, washer and axle nut.

RIM BRAKES

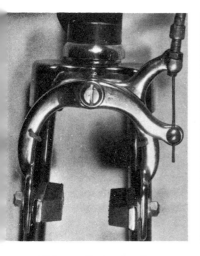

Side-pull rim brake

Center-pull rim brake

A geared bike uses rim brakes. These can stop the bike much faster than a coaster brake can. A rim brake clamps the rim between two rubber brake blocks. The most popular (cheaper) one here is the side-pull type.

Adjusting Side-Pull Type

Adjusting Center-Pull Type

Loosen the lock nut. Then unscrew this adjuster till cable pulls brake blocks to 3/16 inch from rim. Tighten the nut. If needed shift cable end in clamp.

Use the cable adjusting barrel if any. Adjust blocks like these 1/8" from rim so: Loosen nut on back of post, m o v e t h e block, tighten the nut.

Unless you are replacing a cable, don't let the end out of the clamp, the frayed end won't thread back in.

Replacing a Cable

Replace any cable that is broken, frayed, rusty, or stiff-working. Show your bike shop the old one.

If the cable is held by a clamp, loosen the clamp nut. Pull out the cable.

Pull the cable nipple away and down from this type of hand lever. Lift it out.

To remove the end at this hand lever, pull the nipple back on the cable. Swing the cable down and out.

Put the new cable on first at the hand lever, in the same way as other came off. Then do the other end.

Hold brake blocks together. With adjuster halfway in, pull cable through clamp. Tighten the clamp nut.

OIL this pivot and where the s p r i n g ends are. Grease the exposed inner cable. Oil the hand lever pivots.

Replacing Brake Blocks

Better replace the whole assembly — rubber, holder, nut, and washer. However, to replace just the rubber:

Undo these nuts, and take off the brake shoes. Adjust the cable to allow for new block thickness.

Drive out the old block. Spread the open end of the block holder by driving in a wedge or center punch.

Drive in each new block. Hammer the open end of the holder enough so the new block can't come out.

Put the shoe on, *closed* end forward, so the rim won't push the block out. Line the block up with rim.

Troubles

The wheel wobbles and rubs the brake. True it up. The brake rubs the tyre — you'll soon need a new tyre! The brake squeaks — sandpaper its glazed surface. One side doesn't come back. Did you oil the pivots and spring tips? Shame! Maybe there is no end play in the pivot, some meathead used a thick separating washer. Or maybe the whole assembly has become twisted in the fork cross piece. Loosen it, turn it into the right position or a bit beyond and tighten. Lastly, if you're desperate, bend the spring up on the lazy side.

SPOKES AND RIMS

Adding Spokes

There is no particular trick to adding a few spokes. If the spoke is broken and the end can be unscrewed out of the nipple (the threaded part in the rim), then the new spoke can be added without deflating the tyre. If the nipple is broken, or the spoke won't come out of it, deflate the tyre, push it aside to uncover the nipple head and put in a new nipple. Be very sure the new spoke is the right length—check it by placing it beside one in the wheel. Entering a front spoke is simple—notice the pattern of spoke heads to show you which direction the spoke should go through the hub flange.

If you have a number of loose spokes, don't tighten them till you have crayoned the rim to find which ones need the most tightening—see next page.

Rim Zigs and Zags in General

Once your spokes were all a bit loose—that didn't seem right, so you just tightened them—and, wow!—the wheel was so warped it would not run through the fork without rubbing. Or the time John left his bike behind the car in the driveway and—well—one wheel was certainly warped. Truing a wheel takes time, but it is not nearly as nasty a job as some others.

A wheel can be wrong in two ways. It can be out of round, egg-shaped, for example, or it can wobble from side to side. If the sideways warp is very bad, deal with it first, then with out-of-round, and then a final adjustment sideways.

Before you start, get a spoke wrench and about six spokes of the right length and nipples. Measure along the spoke from the rim surface to the spoke head in the hub.

Now take the wheel off, remove the tyre, tube and rim strip, and put the wheel back loosely in the frame. An old front fork clamped in a vice makes a swell wheel holder for this job. Use a screwdriver for nipple adjustment if possible, otherwise use a spoke wrench.

You will find some spokes are rusted into the nipples and must be replaced. Cut the rusted ones near the hub so they come out easily.

1   Spoke needed, sprocket side. If the sprocket lacks holes or slot, remove the sprocket, see pp. 49, 66. If there IS a slot, line it up with the spoke hole and space between brake arm and fork, to enter the spoke from the INSIDE face of the hub flange.

2   If the spoke must enter from OUTSIDE the hub, lead it through the sprocket slot, spoke hole, then above the intersection of the opposite spokes. See the arrow.

To remove a freewheel sprocket cluster, see p. 120.

3 Pull it through, flex it and lead it between other spokes to its nipple.

4 If the spoke pokes above the rim surface, cut off the extra length.

5 & 6 Screw the nipple onto the spoke with the spoke wrench. If the tyre is off or deflated, it is easier to engage the slotted head of the nipple with a screwdriver.

TRUING A RIM

Correcting "Out-of-Round"

This is usually caused by someone tightening spokes without regard to what is happening to the rim. This nitwit effort may also poke some of the spokes through the rim too far—puncture coming up!

When the wheel is not in a true circle, it has a hump or flat spot, usually both. As some spokes must always be loosened before any can be tightened, the flat spot must be found first, and its spokes loosened. Then the hump is found and its spokes tightened. The rim can move 1/8 inch radially for 7 turns of the spoke nipples. Flat spots and humps are shown up by spinning the wheel while holding a crayon or chalk near the proper place.

These operations will probably cause sideways warp, as quite a few turns of the spokes may be needed, and warp can be caused by quite a small adjustment (1/2—1 turn) of the spokes. Final adjustment for warp is therefore done last and has little or no effect on circular shape.

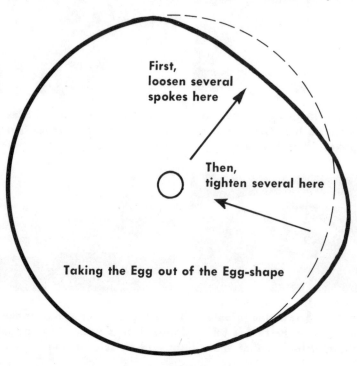

First, loosen several spokes here

Then, tighten several here

Taking the Egg out of the Egg-shape

1 Locate the flat spot by crayoning the inside surface of the rim close to the nipples.

2 Markings on both sides occurring in the same place on the rim show a flat spot.

3 Loosen all the spokes in the marked area, middle ones most.

4 Now find the hump by crayoning the outside of the rim, both edges.

5 If both marks show in the same part, a hump is indicated.

6 Tighten the spokes in the marked stretch, the middle ones most.

Mark the rim again (wipe off the first marks, or use a different coloured crayon), and again loosen any flat spot, pull in any hump. Keep on till it's within 1/16 inch or better of a true circle. This tolerance can be seen in the greatest clearance between the crayon and the rim when the crayon is held so it just touches the remaining hump.

Correcting Sideways Wobble

Sideways wobble is a common rim ailment. If the wheel will still run through the fork, we ignore it. But it is not really hard to put right. The idea is to locate the bumps by crayoning, loosen spokes on the bump side and then tighten on the other side. Theoretically, loosening spokes on one side one turn, and tightening on the other side one turn will shift a 26-inch rim about 1/8 inch sideways. So the middle of a bump 1/8 inch high should be so treated, tapering off to nothing for the spokes at the ends of the bump. Actually, the spokes are not usually found to be equally tight; there is no point in loosening a spoke already very loose, nor in tightening one already tight. So use that thing on your shoulders, one thing it's meant for is thinking. Use it also to decide which rim side actually has the bump—in general, short marks indicate it.

Loosen on the right, tighten on the left, and the rim moves left.

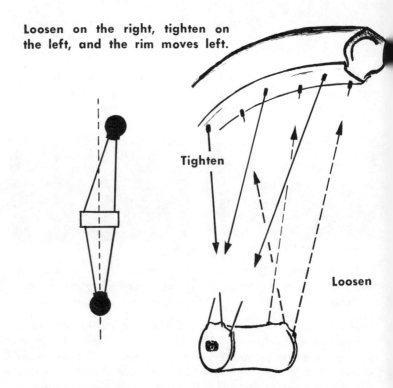

Tighten

Loosen

Let's go. Be sure to loosen spokes before tightening any.

76

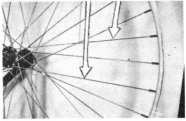

1 To show the bumps, spin the wheel and hold a crayon or chalk close to both sides.

2 Now loosen the spokes that go to the same side of the hub as the mark is on the rim.

3 And tighten the spokes on the other side. Keep at it until the wobble is 1/16 inch or less.

4 If the bump persists (check by crayoning), use the Knee Action method, as the rim is actually bent.

A bike wheel run over by a car may be salvageable if it is not squashed or sharply bent. But it takes "knee action" and considerable time. The result is not as strong as a new rim, as the spokes are at different tensions to hold the rim true. Better get a new rim or wheel.

About straightening a bent rim—if you overdo the knee action by having your hands too far apart, and a number of spokes are loose, the wheel suddenly snaps into a strange pretzel figure. This adds variety but not progress; but the wheel can be snapped back into shape without damage.

Wheels with Sprocket Clusters

Spokes on the right-hand side are tighter than the others to "dish" the wheel. The rim must be centered between the lock nuts, not centered on the hub.

REBUILDING WHEELS

You can send in your hub to a mail-order house or a bike repair shop and have a new wheel built on it—be sure to say what size. If you are willing to spend some time on it, try it yourself. If a wheel is to be rebuilt when installing a new coaster brake, for example, then 36 spokes of the correct length and nipples are required and all must be similar. The old spokes are first cut away, cutting them close to the hub. All the spokes are threaded through the hub in the direction required. When all the spokes are threaded into the flange, the whole thing is laid on a table with the spokes radiating out from the hub and the rim is laid at the ends of the spokes.

Then follow another wheel to get the pattern right; start the 9 spokes coming from one side of one flange into every fourth hole in the rim engaging the spoke by one turn of the nipple. Be sure that the set of rim holes is on the same side of the rim as the hub flange concerned. Then start the next set of 9 in their proper holes; be very sure that the pattern is right and that the spokes lie over or under the first lot as required, then follow up with the other two lots of 9 spokes each. At this stage all of the spokes will be entered in the rim and all held by one turn of the nipples

Now tighten all nipples by six turns each. If all the spokes were identical in length and all nipples were identical in their thread length, then the wheel could be made true by merely tightening all nipples the same number of turns; but in our experience, these parts are not identical and this system works only up to a certain point. After the total of 7 turns of the nipples, the spokes should still be on the loose side, at least most of them will be. Now proceed to tighten up nipples possibly one or two more turns each if they call for it, but in any case, the end of all spokes should be the same distance down in the nipple from the screwdriver slot. Work around the whole wheel to obtain this condition and if compatible, to obtain the same degree of tightness on the spokes.

Now test the wheel for roundness and freedom from wobble as described under "Truing a Rim" and correct it by the methods given. Simple wasn't it—or was it?

TOOLS FOR COASTER BRAKE BIKES

Ordinary wrenches in inch sizes fit most U.S. bikes and those made for U.S. British bikes usually take Whitworth or metric wrenches. Continental and Japanese things like derailleurs take metric wrenches, see p. 105.

1. Useful tools for a bike, and later for a car!
A. Thin wrench, 1/2 and 9/16″.   B. Box/open-end wrenches 7/16, 1/2, 9/16, 5/8″. If possible, get a whole set from 3/8 to 3/4″.   C. Adjustable 8-inch open-end wrench. A monkey wrench is also useful.   D. "Dumbell" wrench. (refers to shape, not to owner), useful for trips.

2. Some special tools. E_1 is for New Departure; E_2 for Perry B-100, Komet, Styria, etc. E_3 for Sturmey Archer; F for Phillips rim brakes. G is for spoke nipples. Other wrenches shown are "universal."

Storing Your Bike — No, this picture is not upside down. These bikes are asleep (like bats) for the winter. They are hung on rubber-tube covered, 4-inch nails driven into the sides of the garage roof joists. This preserves the finish and tyres, and keeps the bikes out of the way.

BIKES WITH 3, 5, OR 10 SPEEDS

Skip this page if you already have a geared bike — gear hub or derailleur.

In the Junior Set, the "in" bike has 3, 5, or even 10 speeds and a shift lever like a Mack truck, so if you're young you want a geared bike mostly because the kid next door has one. But read on, and think! If your hands are big enough to grasp rim brake levers, well, maybe. If you take really good care of a bike, OK. But if you bang a bike around, let it fall and loan it to "friends," then accept our sympathy — you'll need it. Your bike will be mostly up for repairs.

Let's get something straight. The more speeds you have does NOT mean the faster you go. A 5-speed bike does NOT go 5 times as fast as a 1-speed one. A choice of speeds, or "gears" allows you to pedal with the least effort, whether up or down hill, with or against the wind. Low gear lets you ride up hills slowly, but it's faster than walking. High gear is fast on down grades or with the wind, and you don't pedal fast either. You can keep up the same pedaling rate or "cadence." On a trip, you soon learn the big difference in effort between coaster brake and geared bikes, whether your muscles are puny, athletic, or rusted.

Geared bikes have "caliper brakes" applied to front and rear wheel rims. The rear hub is too busy with other things to have a coaster brake. Rim brakes can stop a bike very suddenly — much quicker than a coaster brake.

Internally Geared Hubs

The best known and widely used geared hub is the British 3-speed Sturmey-Archer. Its internal workings are described in the next few pages. Low gear makes the wheel turn slower than the sprocket. In normal or 2nd gear, wheel and sprocket turn at the same speed. High or 3rd gear drives the wheel faster than the sprocket. Gear shifting is done through a little chain pulled out of the hollow axle by a cable.

The popular model is the AW. There are other hubs differing in gear ratios. There is also a 4-speed and a 5-speed job, S5 with two controlling cables. There is even a 3-speed unit with a coaster brake in it.

Service instructions are given here for the A.W. Instructions for the others are available from Raleigh dealers. The Wheelgoods Corp. catalog "Handbook of Cycl-ology" (see p. 109) includes service information on AW, SW, TCW Mark III, and S5.

Shimano (Japanese) also make a 3-speed gear hub and a 2-speed one which is shifted by slight back pedaling. Both of these are also made with built-in coaster brakes. The 2- and 3-speed hubs are also offered combined with a 4-speed derailleur to give 8- and 12-speed hubs.

Derailleurs

A derailleur is an amazing bit of mechanism. What it does sounds impossible but it works, and works well. It makes a bike chain jump from one sprocket to another! The usual rear wheel derailleur operates on five sprockets, from small to large. The large one gives "low gear," the small sprocket gives "high gear."

The derailleur levers move two rollers in a "chain cage" sideways, which leads the chain to the sprocket you want. This chain cage is kept parallel to the sprockets by a lever parallelogram (look it up, stupid). As you pedal, the chain jumps on to the sprocket next the chain cage.

The chain cage is spring-loaded so it can swing and adjust the length of chain for each sprocket. The upper roller in the cage, next the sprocket, is called a "jockey" wheel or roller. The lower roller is called the "tension" wheel. Derailleur chains are longer and narrower than others and don't have removable links.

The rear sprocket cluster is often referred to as a "freewheel" since its hub contains a freewheeling device.

Many touring and racing bikes also have two (even three) sprockets called "chainwheels" of slightly different size at the pedal crank. A "front derailleur" puts the chain on one or other sprocket. Two front sprockets, combined with the five rear ones, give you ten "gears" or "speeds."

So a 5-speed bike is one with 5 rear sprockets and rear derailleur, a 10-speed also has two chainwheels and front derailleur. For the mature rider, there are many beautiful, lightweight, high precision 5- and 10-speed bikes. They are a pleasure to own and a delight to ride.

STURMEY ARCHER 3-SPEED HUBS

This applies mostly to their AW hub, in part to their other hubs, and even to similar 3-speeds hubs like the J. C. Higgins, B.S.A., Brampton, etc.

Add only Sturmey-Archer oil through the lubricator every two weeks.

Adjusting Gearshifts, Various Models

AW, AB, AG, TCW Mk III

FW, FM, FC, FG, SW

Normal gear—shoulder on indicator rod is flush with end of axle. If not: (Check bearings first).

Left end of indicator rod (Is it screwed in tight?) is flush with left end of axle, for normal gear.

Adjust anchor which holds end of cable. (First set control lever at normal.)

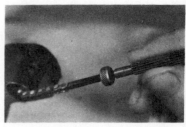

For a small adjustment, loosen this nut, turn this sleeve till shoulder is in right place. Lock the nut.

You can check some gearshifts this way: Rest your hand on a pedal. Shift the lever slowly from high to normal to low. The pedal should let go about halfway between lever positions. You can adjust the shift accordingly, but first check the right-hand cone—see next page. This cone affects the indicator rod position.

Replacing Cable

Detach wire from chain at hub. Pull back and unscrew this ferrule.

Put control in Low position. Push wire through to detach it from its slot.

With lever next handlebar, pull wire out. If needed, raise spring-held pawl.

Push new wire through same way, catch wire end in slot with lever in Low.

Adjusting Bearings

Adjust only the left side. Loosen axle nut, locknut. (If right cone was moved, loosen left cone, finger tighten right cone, back ½ turn, tighten locknut.)

Finger tighten left cone, back up ¼ turn. Tighten locknut. There must be a little side play at wheel rim. Readjust if needed. This adjusts all bearings.

How a Three-Speed Hub Works
IN PARTICULAR, THE STURMEY ARCHER AW

Internally geared hubs, as the name implies, have all the working parts inside the hub shell. Different speeds are obtained by a planetary gear system, explained below. One speed is slower than that of the sprocket, one equal to it, and the third is faster than the sprocket. Gear shifting is done by a sliding clutch which engages the drive wanted, and disengages the other two.

1. GEARS. The "sun" gear (on the axle), "planet" gears (around it), and gear ring (around them) are the heart of any multi-speed hub. The planet gear axles are held in the "planet cage" (not shown). This gear system provides a difference in speed between rotating parts, so:

In this hub, the sun gear is held stationary on the axle. As the planet cage turns, its planet gears, being meshed with the fixed sun gear, must turn on their axles. Therefore, their outer teeth must turn faster than the cage. The gear ring must rotate with these gear teeth, that is, *always* faster than the planet cage. Let's see how we use these facts.

84

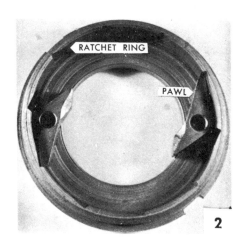

2

2. PAWLS. Both the planet cage and the gear ring carry pawls which ratchet inside the two ends attached to the hub shell. So the pawls B on the faster part, the gear ring, always drive the shell unless disengaged from it. In this case, the slower part, the planet cage, drives the shell by its pawls.

3

3. GEAR SELECTOR. The sprocket is attached to a four-pronged "driver." A cross-shaped "sliding clutch" can move along the driver, as positioned by the small rod attached by the small chain to the control cable. The position of this clutch determines which part of the pawl cage or gear ring it drives.

HIGH GEAR

The sliding clutch, shown here out of its driver, is at left end of its travel, and is driving the planet cage. But the planet cage is driving the gear ring faster than itself. So the pawls on the gear ring (not shown) drive the hub, which therefore rotates faster than the sprocket.

You can now see why a broken or loose cable puts the hub in high gear. There is a spring forcing the sliding clutch toward the planet cage.

NORMAL GEAR

The sliding clutch is pulled away from the planet cage, and drives dogs (bumps!) attached to the gear ring. The pawls B on the gear ring drive the hub shell. So, now the wheel rotates at the same speed as the sprocket. Notice that in normal gear, the driving force does not go through the gears at all.

The ticking sound in high and normal gears comes from the left ratchet ring of the hub shell running faster than the spring-urged pawls A.

LOW GEAR

The sliding clutch is pulled farther to the right, to engage a second set of dogs in the gear ring. In this case, the outer ends of the sliding clutch push out the back end of the pawls, so the forward ends do not drive the hub shell. So, the slower moving pawls A on the planet cage do drive the shell. So, the wheel rotates slower than the clutch, driver, and sprocket. As only the one set of pawls A is in action, there is no ticking sound.

Exploded View, AW Hub

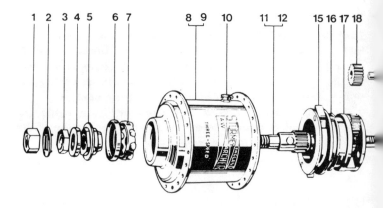

(1) Low gear — 25 % decrease
(2) Normal gear — direct drive
(3) High gear — 33 1/3 % increase

Parts List

Photo No.	Sales No.	Description
1	HMN 128	L.H. Axle Nut
2	HMW 145	Axle Lock Washer
3	HMN 132	Lock Nut
4	HMW 129	Axle Washer, $\frac{1}{8}''$ (3.2 m.m.) thick
5	HSA 101	Cone with Dust Cap
6	HSA 102	Outer Dust Cap
7	HSA 103	Ball Cage (with Ball Bearings)
8	HSA 104	Shell – 40 hole – and Ball Cup Combined
9	HSA 105	Shell – 36 hole – and Ball Cup Combined
10	HSA 106	Lubricator (Plastic)
11	HSA 107	Axle – $5\frac{3}{4}''$ (146 m.m.)
12	HSA 108	Axle – $6\frac{1}{4}''$ (159 m.m.)
15	HSA 111	Low Gear Pawl
16	HSA 112	Pawl Pin
17	HSA 113	Planet Cage
18	HSA 115	Planet Pinion
19	HSA 114	Pinion Pin
20	HSA 116	Clutch Sleeve
21	HSA 117	Clutch
22	HSA 118	Gear Ring

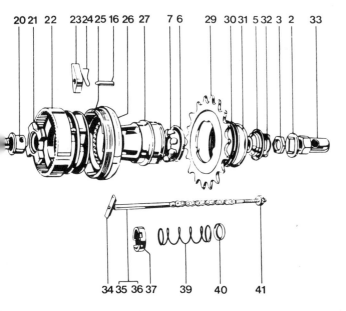

Parts List

Photo No.	Sales No.	Description
23	HSA 119	Gear Ring Pawl
24	HSA 120	Pawl Spring
25	HSA 121	R.H. Ball Ring
26	HSA 122	Inner Dust Cap
27	HSA 123	Driver
29	HSL 716/ HSL 720 HSL 722	Sprocket, 16-20 plus 22T
30	HMW 127	Sprocket Spacing Washer (2 off)
31	HSL 721	Sprocket Circlip
32	HMW 147	Cone Lockwasher
33	HMN 129	R.H. Axle Nut
34	HSA 124	Axle Key
35	HSA 125	Indicator Coupling – $5\frac{3}{4}''$ (146 m.m.) Axle
36	HSA 126	Indicator Coupling – $6\frac{1}{4}''$ (159 m.m.) Axle
37	HSA 127	Thrust Ring
39	HSA 128	Clutch Spring
40	HSA 129	Clutch Spring Cap
41	HMN 134	Indicator Coupling Connection Lock Nut

To Dismantle the AW Hub

1. Remove the left-hand cone locknut with any spacing washers noting their order, so that they may be re-assembled
2. Remove left-hand cone.
3. Unscrew right-hand ball ring from hub shell, using hammer and punch, and withdraw internals as a complete unit. The notches of the R.H. ball ring should be examined for the letters SA and a piece of string or adhesive tape attached to spoke adjacent to the marked notch. The reason for this is that the R.H. ball ring has a two start thread and must be replaced in the same position to avoid having to retrue the wheel
4. If it is necessary to remove the sprocket from the driver prise off the circlip. The spacing washers, sprocket and outer dustcap may then be lifted off the driver. There must always be two $\frac{1}{16}''$ spacing washers. Note their position and also whether sprocket offset is facing inwards or outwards, as they must all be put back to maintain original chain line.
5. Remove the low gear pawls, pins and springs.
6. Place the left-hand end of the axle in a vice and remove the right-hand locknut, washers if any, cone lock washer and cone, noting their arrangement so that they may be replaced in order.
7. Lift off in the following order, the clutch spring, the driver, the right-hand ball ring and the gear ring.
8. Remove the gear ring pawls, pins and springs.
9. Remove the thrust ring and washer, unscrew the indicator rod
10. Push out the axle key and remove the sliding clutch and sleeve.
11. Lift off the planet cage and remove planet pinions and pins.
12. If necessary, because of a worn bearing surface or ratchets, the left-hand ball cup may be removed from a hub shell. It has a left-hand thread.
13. The channel-section dust caps in the left-hand ball cup and driver are a press-in fit. If a new ball retainer and balls have to be fitted it is recommended that a new dust cap is fitted

POINTS TO CHECK

1. Freedom of sliding clutch in driver. This should slide easily.
2. Axle between centres for truth.
3. All gear teeth for wear or chipping.
4. All races for wear or pitting (6 in all).
5. Pinion pins, sliding clutch and gear ring splines for rounding off on engagement points.
6. Pawls and Pawl Ratchets for wear.

To Assemble the AW Hub

1. If the left-hand ball cup has been removed from the hub shell replace it by screwing anti-clockwise.
2. Fit the pawls, pins and springs into the gear ring as follows:—
Place the gear ring, with the teeth downwards, on a flat surface.

Place a pawl spring along the side of a pawl so that the loop is over the pin hole and the foot is under the long nose of the pawl. While holding a pawl pin ready in the left hand, grip the nose of the pawl and the foot of the spring between the thumb and forefinger of the right hand and slide the pawl, tail first, between the flanges of the gear ring. When the hole in the pawl and the loop in the spring coincide with the holes in the flanges, push the pawl pin into position.

Smear grease in the channels of the dust caps of the left-hand ball cup and driver and in the recess of the right-hand ball ring. *Do not use grease anywhere else.*

Hold the left-hand end of the axle in a vice so that the slot for the axle key is above the sun pinion, and fit the planet cage.

Add the planet pinions and pins. (The small ends of the pins protrude).

Fit the sleeve (flange first), the sliding clutch with the recess on the flange of the sleeve, and the axle key (with the flat of the key facing upwards), and screw in the indicator rod to hold them

Fit the thrust ring and washer, making sure that the flatted ends of the key engage properly in the slots of the thrust ring.

Fit the previously prepared gear-ring sub-assembly.

Fit the right-hand ball-ring complete with inner dust cap (24 $\frac{3}{16}''$ balls).

Fit the driver complete with ball cage.

Drop the clutch spring over the axle.

Screw up the right-hand cone finger-tight. Then slacken it back half a turn and lock it in that position with the special washer and locknut. *On no account must the cone be unscrewed more than half a turn, as that would throw the gear mechanism out of adjustment.*

Reverse the assembly in the vice and fit the planet-cage pawls. *To replace pawls and springs in the planet cage.*

Place a pawl between the flanges, with the flat driving edge pointing towards the right, and insert a pawl pin through the outside flange and half-way through the pawl. With tweezers grip the bent leg of the pawl spring and pass the spring along the under side of the pawl until the loop of the spring is in line with the hole through the pawl and both legs of the spring are between the pawl and the planet cage. The pawl pin can now be pushed right in. If the job has been done correctly, the pawls will be pointing towards the right, with the driving edge uppermost.

4. Remove the assembled mechanism from the vice and pour about two teaspoonfuls of Sturmey-Archer oil into the planet cage.

5. The gear unit is now inserted vertically upwards into shell and R.H. ball ring screwed in (this has two-start R.H. thread). Note that S.A. mark should line up with marked spoke.

6. Fit the left-hand cone, washers (if any), and locknut in the arrangement noted when dismantling, and adjust the hub bearings.

91

General Notes: It is important that the axle should be prevent
from turning in the chainstay slots, and the flats on the axle a
provided for this purpose. If the fork ends are too wide for t
axle, special washers can be supplied.

If the hub has been disturbed, check the indicator which screws in
the axle key, to ensure that it is in its proper position. It should
screwed up as far as it will go and then turned back just sufficient
line up with the control wire. Note that to do this it need never
turned back more than half a turn.

FAULT FINDING CHART FOR AW GEAR

Note—The major cause of trouble is faulty gear adjustment. Chec
to see that the outer shoulder of the indicator is level with end
axle when gear control is in No. 2 position. If the complai
is sluggish gear change or stiffness, this may point to lack of o
Hub and control should be oiled and re-tested before going furthe
If the fault persists, the following chart should locate the troubl

SYMPTOM	FAULT	REMEDY
No low gear (1st) ..	1. Low gear pawls upside down	1. Fit correctly.
	2. Thrust collar not seating over axle key	2. Fit correctly.
	3. Incorrect axle spring ..	3. Replace.
Slipping in low gear (1st)	1. Sliding clutch worn	1. Replace.
	2. Indicator not screwed home fully	2. Re-adjust.
	3. R.H. cone wrongly adjusted	3. Re-adjust.
	4. Kinks in trigger wire ..	4. Replace.
	5. Twisted indicator chain ..	5. Replace.
Fluctuating between 1st gear and 2nd gear	1. Worn gear ring pawls	1. Replace.
Slipping in normal gear (2nd) ..	1. Gear ring dogs and/or clutch worn	1. Replace.
	2. Indicator not screwed home fully	2. Re-adjust.
Slipping in top gear (3rd)	1. Pinion pins and/or clutch worn	1. Replace.
	2. Very weak or distorted axle spring	2. Fit new spring.
	3. Incorrect R.H. cone adjustment	3. Re-adjust.
	4. Grit between clutch sleeve and axle	4. Clean.
Hub runs stiffly. Drag on pedals ..	1. Too many balls in ball ring	1. Fit 24 only.
	2. Cones excessively tight ..	2. Re-adjust.
	3. Chainstay ends not parallel	3. Correct.
	4. Corrosion	4. Clean and use Sturmey-Archer o
	5. Distorted dust caps ..	5. Replace.
Sluggish gear change	1. Distorted axle spring · ..	1. Replace.
	2. Bent axle	2. Replace.
	3. Worn toggle chain link ..	3. Replace.
	4. Guide pulley out of line ..	4. Re-align.
	5. Lack of oil, or frayed wire ..	5. Oil or replace.

GETTING OUT OF TROUBLE

or Getting Home the Hard Way

Trousers caught in chain. Walk the bike backward, turning the pedals backward. Going forward will wreck trousers and chain.

Puncture, no patch kit. Try patching with ends, not middle of Band-aid or masking tape or Scotch tape. Maybe several layers of postage stamps would hold. (Will an air mail stamp hold air?)

Run into something? If the front wheel hits the bike frame, straighten the fork — see p. 28. (No, running backwards into something else won't fix it.)

Broken Sturmey-Archer cable. You still have high gear. If you have any wire like a paper clip, pull the little control chain out, put the clip through a link to hold it out. This gives you second gear, but pedal gently, gear engagement is not accurate.

Broken or stuck derailleur cable. You still have high gear. You can also get the next or even middle gear if you run the high gear screw all the way in, first removing its holding spring.

Broken chain. Thumb your way home. Maybe another rider can tow you. IF you can drive out the two roller pins on either side of the break, and IF you have wire and a pliers, MAYBE you can improvise a repair.

Need a car pick up? Tell the driver to bring an adjustable wrench so you can loosen the handlebar and remove the front wheel. Then you can get the bike into a car boot.

Tourniquet used to straighten bent fork.

SHIMANO 3-SPEED HUB

The Shimano 3-speed hub, FA type is an internally geared hub. It uses planetary gears, which are explained on previous pages. However, the Shimano hub is quite different in its internal structure.

Hub shells are supplied for 28, 36, and 40 spokes. Sprockets are available in 16, 18, 19, 20, 21, and 22 teeth, and are dished to allow chain alignment.

In this hub the gear ratios are high (H) 1.33, normal (N) 1.00, and low (L) 0.75.

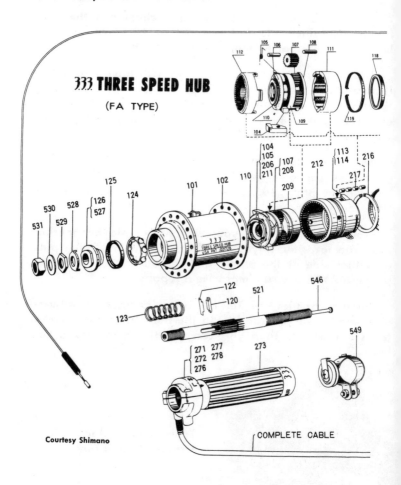

333 THREE SPEED HUB
(FA TYPE)

COMPLETE CABLE

Courtesy Shimano

Gear shifting is done by twist grip, or on junior bikes by "Click-Stick" lever. Click-Sticks have a barrel adjustment for the cable.

Adjusting the gearshift is very simple, see the next page. It's also easy to replace a broken cable. However, if you're a beginner, don't try to overhaul the internal hub mechanism. Leave it to experts. Or you'll have enough bits left for a cuckoo clock.

Shimano also makes a 3-speed hub with coaster brake, the Tri-Matic. There are also Shimano 2-speed hubs, with and without coaster brakes. Gears are changed on these by slight back pedaling.

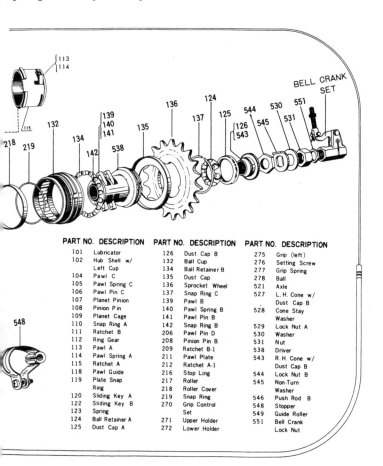

PART NO.	DESCRIPTION	PART NO.	DESCRIPTION	PART NO.	DESCRIPTION
101	Lubricator	126	Dust Cap B	275	Grip (left)
102	Hub Shell w/ Left Cup	132	Ball Cup	276	Setting Screw
		134	Ball Retainer B	277	Grip Spring
104	Pawl C	135	Dust Cap	278	Ball
105	Pawl Spring C	136	Sprocket Wheel	521	Axle
106	Pawl Pin C	137	Snap Ring C	527	L. H. Cone w/ Dust Cap B
107	Planet Pinion	139	Pawl B		
108	Pinion Pin	140	Pawl Spring B	528	Cone Stay Washer
109	Planet Cage	141	Pawl Pin B		
110	Snap Ring A	142	Snap Ring B	529	Lock Nut A
111	Ratchet B	206	Pawl Pin D	530	Washer
112	Ring Gear	208	Pinion Pin B	531	Nut
113	Pawl A	209	Ratchet B-1	538	Driver
114	Pawl Spring A	211	Pawl Plate	543	R. H. Cone w/ Dust Cap B
115	Ratchet A	212	Ratchet A-1		
118	Pawl Guide	216	Stop Ling	544	Lock Nut B
119	Plate Snap Ring	217	Roller	545	Non-Turn Washer
		218	Roller Cover		
120	Sliding Key A	219	Snap Ring	546	Push Rod B
122	Sliding Key B	270	Grip Control Set	548	Stopper
123	Spring			549	Guide Roller
124	Ball Retainer A	271	Upper Holder	551	Bell Crank Lock Nut
125	Dust Cap A	272	Lower Holder		

Adjusting the Shimano Gearshift

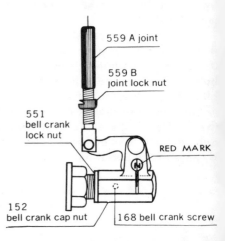

To adjust for N: Undo joint lock nut. Turn sleeve (joint) to bring red N in hole, line in slot. Tighten lock nut.

559 A joint

559 B joint lock nut

551 bell crank lock nut

RED MARK

152 bell crank cap nut

168 bell crank screw

If the bell crank was off the axle: Be sure the push rod 546 is in. Add the lock nut 551 loosely. Screw the bell crank cap nut on until its screw 168 touches the axle end. If needed, back up slightly to line up the cable. Tighten the lock nut. Adjust as above. Ride the bike, shift gears, ending at N. Readjust if needed.

Note: Twist grip may show N incorrectly. Soft cement or hard use may rotate grip on its cylinder. Slacken cable completely, turn the twist grip to feel three notches. Center one is N. Use it to set the bell crank.

To Replace a Cable.

1   Detach the cable from the bell crank. Undo these two screws to remove the cap while you hold lower part.

2   Lower the bottom part without losing the ball or spring under it. Pull out enough cable to lift it free of the slot, move the cable end along and out.

BENDIX 2-SPEED AUTOMATIC

See description on next page

Taking It Apart

Lacking special wrench AB-102, make one from 3/8″ water pipe so it fits lock nut AB-35. Hold cone with a wrench, loosen and remove lock nut. To remove cone, turn sprocket forward, (clockwise.) If it stops, turn back and go forward again. Keep turning sprocket forward till cone stops unscrewing. Then unscrew and remove cone. Unscrew and remove sprocket, with related parts. Remove ball retainer. Remove brake assembly and clutches from other side. Clean everything in paraffin.

Unhook end of coupling AB-21 from slots of low speed drive clutch AB-303. Also unhook it from ends of spring on high speed drive clutch AB-23.

To separate the low speed clutch AB-303 and drive end expander AB-306 pry up top side of retarder spring AB-312 and peel it off. Easy!

CHECK for wear and replace parts that show excessive wear, mutilation, or rough bearing surfaces. Check these: Brake surfaces. Knurled clutch surfaces. Clutch internal threads and driving screw threads. Slots of retarder coupling AB-21. All indexing spring prongs. Damaged indexing sleeve (replace whole driving screw).

Bendix 2-Speed Automatic with Shoe Brakes

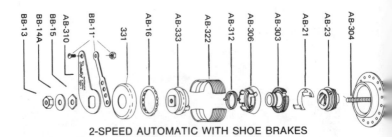

BB-13
BB-14A
BB-15
AB-310
BB-11
331
AB-16
AB-333
AB-322
AB-312
AB-306
AB-303
AB-21
AB-23
AB-304

2-SPEED AUTOMATIC WITH SHOE BRAKES

This 2-speed unit changes from one gear to the other by slight back pedaling. Further back pedaling applies a coaster brake. Three models were made: a "Red-Band" with multiple disc brake, "Yellow Band" shoe brakes, shown here, and a "Blue Band" overdrive type with shoe brakes.

Two speeds come from two driving screws. The high-speed one (in Red and Yellow Band types) makes the wheel turn at the same rate as the sprocket. The low-speed one is geared to the sprocket by planetary gears and turns the wheel slower than the sprocket. The indexing

1 This indexing spring goes over the indexing sleeve. Prong A, inside high-speed clutch, allows spring to turn only in arrow direction. Prong B engages stops D1, D2, etc. of the indexing sleeve. When sprocket turns backward, stop D1 turns down and slips under prong B, ending at position D2.

2 Indexing spring is at one of 6 D-stops so prong C, at pencil point comes at one of three notches of high-speed

98

Order of disassembly from the right

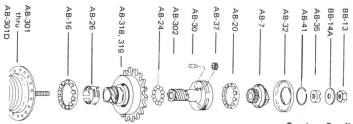

AB-301
thru
AB-301D

AB-301

AB-16

AB-26

AB-318, 319

AB-24

AB-302

AB-30

AB-37

AB-20

AB-7

AB-32

AB-41

AB-35

BB-14A

BB-13

spring controls which screw is driving.

When this spring lets the high speed clutch run all the way up its driving screw it engages the hub shell and drives it. When the spring holds the high speed clutch out a bit, the low speed clutch runs up its driving screw and engages a different part of the hub shell. The low speed clutch can't engage the hub shell when the high speed clutch is driving. This is because the shell is turning faster than the low speed clutch is.

Now let's see how it works — read it twice!

clutch, so this clutch can screw in all the way. At this clutch position the outer serrated part engages the inside of the hub shell, not shown.

3 Back pedaling moves clutch out. Pedaling forward again rotates spring 1/6 turn and pulls clutch in. Now prong C doesn't come at a notch. It holds high-speed clutch out, doesn't let it engage hub shell. Low-speed clutch screws in and engages a different part of hub shell.

Reassembling Bendix 2-Speed Automatic

Pack ball retainers with ball-bearing grease. Except as noted, apply grease also to all internal parts, including the axle where it comes inside the driving screws. Put SAE20 or 30 oil on the inside knurled surface of the high speed clutch, on the triple threads of clutches and driving screws, and on the indexing sleeve. In flat country the disc pack can be lightly lubricated. In hilly country use lots of heat-resistant grease such as Texaco Starfax No. 2.

1   Hold l. s. clutch AB-303 like so, add part AB-306 so teeth meet. (don't yours?).

2   If retarder spring AB-312 was off, pry it back into groove of expander.

3   Hook coupling AB-21 on retarder spring of h.s. clutch AB-23, low slot over low hook of spring.

4   Hook coupling AB-21 into slots of low speed driving clutch AB-303.

5   Put indexing spring AB-26 on sleeve of drive screw, 3 short lugs next ball race.

6   Put 11 greased balls AB-24 into ball race of high-speed driving screw.

7 Put low-speed driver AB-328 in high-speed driver.

8 Put this assembly into the hub, large hole side.

9 Put brake shoes AB-322 into hub around expander. Add axle-brake arm assembly, turn until expander seats.

10 Put ball retainer AB-16 in hub shell, flat side out. Hold both driving screws, screw clockwise into hub.

11 Put ball retainer AB-20 in l.s. driver, flat side out. Turn adjusting cone and sun gear AB-7 until it touches planet gears. Keep turning it, turn sprocket other way.

12 When the cone bottoms, turn it back ¼ turn. Hold it there, add and tighten lock nut AB-35. Readjust if needed for slight side play at the wheel rim.

All Bendix brake parts should be ordered through a bicycle dealer. Bendix does not accept direct orders.

DERAILLEUR ADJUSTMENTS

Adjusting a Rear Derailleur

Your derailleur has been working nicely; then, either suddenly or gradually, it won't shift to low gear (large sprocket) or maybe not to high gear. Maybe neither . . . What happened?

Sudden change: either the derailleur got bashed out of line or some meathead fooled with the adjustments.

Gradual change: the cable stretched (they all do) or the pivots of the derailleur need oil. A slack cable won't pull the derailleur all the way in to the largest sprocket. If too tight, the cable won't let the derailleur move out as far as the smallest sprocket.

Oil is vital. Because of the many pivots, an oil-less derailleur is sticky and won't move as far as the small sprocket, even with a slack cable. A dry chain also resists shifting. Use cycle oil, not household or penetrating oil.

Doing a complete cleanup and lube job means taking off the wheel and chain. Removing the wheel is easier if the chain is on the smallest sprocket. Removing the chain needs the rivet tool (DON'T use a removable link). See the section on chains, which includes a lube job. Clean the derailleur and sprockets with toothbrush and paraffin used sparingly. Keep it off the tyre, and absorb spatter. Dry with paper towels. Then use oil, wipe off excess. Grease the cables where they leave their sheaths.

Here we show you in pictures how to put the adjustments right, but a derailleur is a complex mechanism. There are deep-seated things that can go wrong and should be put right by an experienced bicycle mechanic. This includes a derailleur badly bashed out of line.

Here is what you do with the bike upside down:

1. First look past the chain cage to make sure it is parallel to the sprockets. If it is slightly out of line and if you can see what is bent, maybe you can straighten it with a wrench. Be careful not to bend the bike frame tips.
2. Oil all the pivots. Grease the cable ends.
3. Tighten the control lever if derailleur shifts itself.
4. Adjust cable length.
5. Adjust high gear adjusting screw.
6. Adjust low gear adjusting screw.

Do these steps in the order given; they usually apply.

How the Adjusting Screws Work

These are stop screws which limit the travel of the levers. The high gear one stops the levers in the outward direction, the other in the inward direction.

If the high gear screw is unscrewed too far, the chain can slip down between sprocket and bike frame. If too far in, the levers can't move the chain to the small sprocket.

If the low gear screw is unscrewed too far, the chain can slip down between large sprocket and wheel. If too far in, the levers can't reach the largest sprocket.

Both screws can vibrate out of adjustment. The pictures show how to adjust them. Make final adjustments after riding. The chain should shift readily and run quietly.

If you do set the adjusting screws, be sure the control lever is in its extreme position (high or low) and that it stays there. When you shift, shift one gear at a time.

If your derailleur isn't shown here and you don't know

which screw is which, do this: after adjusting the cable, put the chain on the smallest sprocket.

Now, squeeze the derailleur levers toward the outside, to contact the high gear screw. Turn each screw.

The one that moves the derailleur is the high gear screw.

Pivots and Cable Can Affect Shifting

The high and low gear screws usually don't need attention on a new bike. You can be misled by sticky pivots. Even with oil, if pivots are too tight, the derailleur won't pull the chain out to the smallest sprocket. Don't blame the high gear screw. If the cable is slightly slack, and you can squeeze the derailleur outward with your fingers, suspect tight pivots. Try loosening the pivot nuts SLIGHTLY —say 1/6 turn.

If shifting is erratic, even with freely working pivots, check the cable itself. Sometimes crudely cut sheath ends bite on the cable wire. Withdraw the wire, cut a good end on the sheath with a fine hack saw. A rusty cable wire is another offender, replace it. For smoothest cable operation, remove the wire entirely, apply medium grease to its whole length, and replace it. Be sure the wire is working freely, with no kinks in wire or sheath.

Adjusting a Front Derailleur

The usual front derailleur is just a cable-operated chain guide with two stop screws. Note: the LARGE sprocket gives high gear, the small one low gear. Just the opposite of the rear sprocket cluster. As on the rear unit, adjust the cable first. Then, if needed, adjust low gear and high gear in that order. Oil on the pivots is vital.

If needed, reposition the front derailleur so that:

1. The chain guide is parallel to the chainwheel.
2. When the chain is on the large front and rear sprockets, it must not touch the chainguide.
3. With the chain on the smallest sprockets, it must not touch the chainguide bushing.
4. The chainguide should clear the large chainwheel by about $1/8$ to $3/16$ inches.

If you move the Huret front derailleur tube clamp, tighten the right side first — very short thread!

If any front derailleur slips on the tube, put folded sandpaper, gritty side out, between tube and clamp.

Does the Chain Skip?

This sometimes happens on the smallest rear sprocket (high gear). Before you assume the chain cage needs more tension, check these:

1. If the bike is new, a chain link may be tight. Invert the bike, run the chain backwards. A tight link will "bobble" over the rollers. Loosen it with the chain rivetting tool used so the pin is pushed slightly away from one side.
2. If the bike is more than a year old, used quite a bit, and the skip occurs only in high gear, the smallest sprocket may be worn. You can't see it easily. Your bike shop can replace that sprocket.

Sprocket Alignment

The middle rear sprocket must line up with the chainwheel on a 5-speed bike; or with the space between chainwheels on a 10-speed bike. Look past the sprocket to check this. The wheel can be tilted a little in the fork tips. It can also be moved sideways with washers. When you remove the back wheel, put it back in the same spot, with the washers where they were.

Misalignment wears sprockets and chain and causes poor derailleur operation and noise.

TOOLS FOR TOURING BIKES

Most derailleurs and rim brakes used here are made in continental Europe or Japan, so you need metric wrenches. Some British bikes take Whitworth wrenches. For bike tool sources, see p. 109. Get their catalogues.

Mafac tool kit. A lightweight compact metric (6-16mm) kit for on-the-road use. Fits derailleurs, brakes, etc.

Freewheel removing tools
Left: spline type
Right: two-lug type

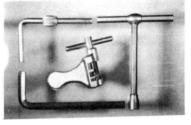

Allen wrenches, 5, 6, and 7mm. (Campagnolo parts.) Chain riveter-extractor.

BernzOmatic metric socket set, 6-12mm, SM-14B. Sold by hardware, department and bigger bike shops. Adjustable 4-inch wrench, 8-inch size is also useful. Cone wrench, 15 - 16mm, 13-14 also from bike shops.

Naturally, you also need pliers, screwdrivers, etc. If you have special problems, the most valuable tool is between your ears. Do try thinking, you'll enjoy it!

HURET ALLVIT DERAILLEUR

In high gear   In low gear

These are made in France, reliable and popular here. One of the "Schwinn approved" derailleurs is an Allvit type. Before you tinker, read the preceding two pages. And don't assume that the gadgets need adjusting if you have not oiled the chain and the derailleur pivots. Maybe only the cable needs adjusting, a new one stretches.

Oiling

Bending Back to Place

1 First clean with paraffin and toothbrush (spatter!). Then oil all four pivots (both sides) and the small wheel bearings. Best job is with wheel and chain off.

2 Don't attempt this unless you're sure main support is bent. Chain cage must be parallel to sprockets. Be careful not to bend fork tips of the bike.

Adjusting the Rear Derailleur

Adjust the cable first, it must be only just slack at the high gear (small sprocket) position. It must be tight enough to pull the chain all the way over to the large sprocket. Now put the bike in high gear and proceed:

1 If the cable is too slack, unscrew this barrel to tighten it. If this won't go far enough, screw it back in and shorten the cable so:

2 Loosen the cable clamp nut and pull the cable through until it's only just slack. Then tighten the clamp nut. Make a final adjustment with the barrel.

3 With the gear lever set all the way in "high" (chain on small sprocket) turn this high gear screw, watching (see photo below) to line up jockey roller with the small sprocket.

4 Now shift to low gear (chain on largest sprocket). Be sure lever stays there. Turn this low gear screw while watching (below) to line up jockey roller with the largest sprocket.

Allvit Derailleur—continued

Chain Tension

Lever Tension

5 If the chain skips*, increase the spring tension on the chain cage. Hold the cage, wind the spring to the next notch. Be firm!

6 If the derailleur just changes gears all by its little self, tighten the thumbscrew on the control lever, just a little.

*Assuming there are no tight chain links, and the sprocket is not worn.

Adjusting the Huret Luxe Front Derailleur

Like the rear one, the front derailleur cable must have just enough slack to let the chain go on the small chainwheel, but must be able to pull the chain over to the large chainwheel. Two adjusting screws limit the travel each way. So, if needed, adjust the cable at the clamp, put the rear derailleur in middle gear and:

7 Put the chain on the small chainwheel (low gear) lever all the way forward. Adjust this low gear screw to center the chain guide over the small chainwheel.

8 Now shift to high gear, lever all the way down. Adjust this high gear screw to center the chain guide over the large chainwheel. Check it out by riding.

USING DERAILLEUR GEARS

1. Keep pedaling as you shift, don't slack up unless the load is very heavy, such as going uphill. Under normal conditions shift any time, but keep pedaling. Shift only one gear at a time.

2. NEVER back pedal during a shift, it will bend or break something and dent your wallet.

3. Don't worry about which gear you're in. Just shift until you get the pedaling speed (cadence) normal for you. DON'T look back at the hub, uh, uh!

4. The secret is keeping cadence —— that pedaling speed normal to you. It will increase with experience.

5. On a trip, use one gear LOWER than the one that feels comfortable at the start. You should not expend much energy to ride. Take it easy and last.

SIMPLEX PRESTIGE DERAILLEURS

These instructions apply to both Prestige and Criterium. Please re-read and follow pages 102-4. Cleaning and lubrication are not repeated here. Let's check cables first.

1   If the cable seems too slack with the chain on the small sprocket, shorten it: Loosen the cable clamp nut and pull e n o u g h cable through until it's only just slack. Then tighten the cable clamp nut.

Adjusting the Rear Prestige Derailleur

2   With lever in "high" (chain on small sprocket) turn this high gear screw to line up jockey roller with the small sprocket.

3   Now shift to low gear (chain on largest sprocket). Turn this low gear screw to line up jockey roller with the largest sprocket.

Adjusting Front Derailleur
(chain on middle rear sprocket)

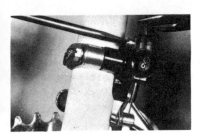

4   The cable must be only just slack at the small chainwheel position. If too slack, loosen this set screw, pull enough cable through and tighten screw. Don't over-tighten — you'll cut the cable!

5   With the chain on the small chainwheel (low gear) loosen this set screw, center chainguide over small chainwheel, tighten screw.

6   Now shift to high gear. Turn this high gear screw to center the chainguide over the large chainwheel. Ride, and readjust if needed.

SHIMANO LARK DERAILLEUR

The Lark resembles others in principle and adjustment. It has a "cable saver" — a spring-loaded cable clamp to prevent damage by a heavy handed meathead. Adjusting screws take either usual or Phillips screwdriver.

Oiling

Greasing Cables

1 First clean with paraffin and toothbrush (spatter!). Then oil all four pivots (both sides and the small wheel bearings. Best job is with wheel and chain off.

2 Apply grease on cable wire where it enters its sheath. Extend cable (high gear position at lower end, in low gear at upper end). Grease other cables too.

Adjusting the Rear Derailleur Cable

The cable must be just barely slack when the bike is in high gear (chain on smallest sprocket). Usually this can be done with the barrel adjustment alone. The cable clamp provides a coarse adjustment if needed. If you do loosen the clamp nut, don't let the cable wire get out of the clamp, the frayed end is almost impossible to thread back in.

3   If the cable seems too slack, unscrew this barrel to tighten it. This should be enough for the first few weeks' cable stretch.

4   If the barrel has a lock nut, tighten it against the post. Some barrels have only springs to hold them from turning.

5   Some "Stick-Shift" controls also have a cable-adjusting barrel on the underside. Use it if needed.

6   If the barrel won't go far enough, run it back in. Loosen the cable clamp nut, pull enough cable through, tighten the nut.

A fairly new bike should not need any derailleur adjustment other than on the cable, if the pivots are working freely (oiled — get it?) But read on. . . .

Adjusting Screws of Shimano Rear Derailleur

7 With the gear lever at the "high" end or "5," (chain on small sprocket) turn this high gear screw. Watch (below) to line up the jockey roller with the small sprocket.

8 Now shift to low gear (largest sprocket). Be sure lever stays put. Adjust this low gear screw while watching (below) to line up the jockey roller with the largest sprocket.

Setting Front Derailleur

The cable must be only just slack at the small chainwheel position. Use the cable clamp to make it so. To position the chainguide: Put and leave the chain on the rear middle sprocket. With the chain still on the small chainwheel, center the chainguide over it by turning low gear screw L. Shift to the large chainwheel and center the chainguide over it by turning high gear screw H. Ride, and readjust if needed.

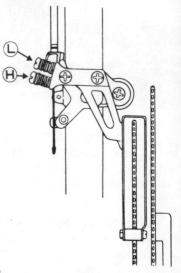

114

CAMPAGNOLO NUOVO RECORD
DERAILLEURS

Campagnolo derailleurs are top flight mechanisms of Italian make. Adjustments are simple and straightforward.

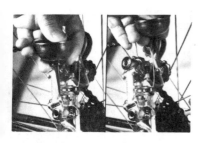

1   First clean with paraffin and toothbrush (old duds!). Then oil all four pivots (do both sides) and small wheel bearings. Best job is with wheel and chain off.

2   Apply grease on cable wire where it enters its sheath. Extend cable (high gear position at lower end, in low gear at upper end). Grease other cables too.

Adjusting the Cable
(Chain on smallest sprocket)

3 If the cable seems too slack with the chain on the small sprocket, shorten it: Loosen the cable clamp bolt and pull e n o u g h cable through until it's only just slack. Then t i g h t e n the cable clamp bolt.

Adjusting the High and Low Gear Screws

A fairly new bike should not need any derailleur adjustment other than on the cable, if the cable and pivots are working freely. But here's how:

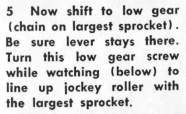

4 With the gear lever set all the way in "high" (chain on small sprocket) watching (see photo below) to line up jockey roller with the small sprocket.

5 Now shift to low gear (chain on largest sprocket). Be sure lever stays there. Turn this low gear screw while watching (below) to line up jockey roller with the largest sprocket.

Final Check. Rotate the pedals to see if the gear shifts quietly and well through all changes. If not, slightly readjust the screws. No other adjustment should be needed.

Adjusting Campagnolo Front Derailleur

The cable must have just enough slack to let the chain go on the small chainwheel, but must be able to pull the chain over to the large chainwheel.

1   If the cable seems too slack with the chain on small chainwheel, shorten it: loosen the cable clamp bolt and pull enough cable through until it's only just slack. Then t i g h t e n the cable clamp bolt.

High and Low Gear Stop Screws

These do not usually need adjusting. But if the front derailleur won't shift properly, and everything is lubricated, put the chain on the rear middle sprocket and:

2   Put the chain on the small c h a i n w h e e l (low gear), lever all the way forward. Adjust this low speed screw to center the chainguide over the small chainwheel.

3   Now shift to high gear, lever all the way down. Adjust this high speed screw to center the chainguide over the large chainwheel, as it appears below.

Check it by riding, using all gears, and readjust if needed.

GT-100 DERAILLEUR

The GT-100 rear derailleur is of conventional parallelogram design. It is used on some Schwinn and other bikes.

Lubrication

Cleaning and oiling are important. To oil pivots, put chain on the large sprocket. Get all 4 pivots, both sides. Grease the cable.

Lever Tension

If the control lever tends to come away from the low gear position, or shifts by itself, tighten the thumbscrew just a little.

Adjusting the Derailleur

Like other derailleurs of Continental origin, it uses metric sized nuts and bolts. The gear adjusting screws take a small Phillips-head screwdriver.

To adjust the cable, shift to high gear (small sprocket) and:

1 If the cable seems too slack, unscrew this barrel to tighten it. If this won't go far enough, screw it back in and shorten the cable so:

2 Loosen the cable clamp nut and pull the cable through until it's only just slack. Tighten the clamp nut. Make a final adjustment with the barrel.

3 With the gear lever set all the way in "high" (chain on small sprocket) turn this high gear screw, watching (see photo below) to line up jockey roller with the small sprocket.

4 Now shift to low gear (chain on largest sprocket). Be sure lever stays there. Adjust this low gear screw while watching (below) to line up jockey roller with the large sprocket.

SCHWINN FRONT DERAILLEUR

Like the rear one, the front derailleur cable must have just enough slack to let the chain go on the small chainwheel, but must be able to pull the chain over to the large chainwheel. Two adjusting screws limit the travel each way. So, if needed, adjust the cable at the clamp, put the rear derailleur in middle gear and:

1   Put the chain on the small chainwheel, lever all the way forward. Adjust this low gear screw to center the chainguide over the small chainwheel.

2   Now shift to high gear, lever all the way down. Adjust this high gear screw to center the chainguide over the large chainwheel. Check it out by riding.

REMOVING A FREEWHEEL (SPROCKET CLUSTER)

A freewheel must come off the hub to clean and oil it or to add spokes on that side. You need a removing tool, which kind depends on the freewheel make. Its name is on its outside, tell your bike shop.

1   Right: Two-lug tool. Left: Internal spline tool.

2   Loosen and remove the spacer nut.

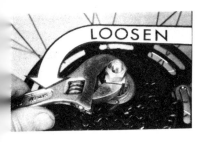

3 To use the spline tool add an axle nut LOOSELY. Loosen and unscrew the freewheel. Lift it off.

4 To use the 2-lug tool add an axle nut TIGHTLY. Loosen the freewheel with a sudden jerk. Then loosen the axle nut and unscrew the freewheel.

5 Run paraffin through to clean, drain and add oil. Don't take the freewheel apart—hard to reassemble. If the high gear sprocket is badly worn (makes the chain skip) have your bike repair man fit a new one.

6 Screw the freewheel back on. Use the spline tool to tighten it, with the axle nut on loosely. Replace the spacer nut, just finger-tight.

7 When you replace a freewheel with a 2-lug tool, tighten it with an axle nut tightly in place.

The spline tool fits most modern freewheels, including those on later Schwinn bikes. There are several types of 2-lug tools, so specify which freewheel you have.

ERRATA

There must be some mistakes, put them here!

NOTES

NOTES

NOTES

NOTES

NOTES

Published by
W. Foulsham & Co. Ltd.
Yeovil Road, Slough, Berks.

Printed in Great Britain by
Redwood Burn Limited
Trowbridge, Wiltshire.